"Take it from a guy who knows what it's like to work a lot of gigs: Dr. Steve Perry, who divides his time between being the planet's most effective school principal and a shake-up-people's-thinking contributor on CNN, is the hardest-working man in the education biz. And that's damn lucky for the thousands of kids who, because of Perry's "serious as a heart attack" approach to education, are now heading off to four-year colleges rather than talking trash on street corners. It's lucky, too, for parents who get to read this amazing book. . . . It's about time someone inside the education system pulled back the curtain on what's lacking, so the common man can help his children get an exceptional education."

—Steve Harvey, author of the #1 *New York Times* bestseller
Act Like a Lady, Think Like a Man

"A leading agitator for reform of the American school system outlines what needs to be done now, and why. Throughout the book, the author displays an admirably action-oriented approach, with plenty of advice for parents and others on how to get involved effectively."

—*Kirkus Reviews*

"Steve Perry is an extraordinary leader and a much-needed voice in the education reform debate. . . . His commitment to improving the lives of children by refusing to accept mediocrity is second to none. In this book, Dr. Perry shows he is willing to do anything to fight for what is most important—our kids."

—Kevin Johnson, mayor of Sacramento, California

PUSH HAS COME TO SHOVE

PUSH HAS COME TO SHOVE

Getting Our Kids the Education They Deserve—
Even If It Means Picking a Fight

DR. STEVE PERRY

CROWN PUBLISHERS
NEW YORK

Copyright © 2011 by Steve Perry, MSW, Ed.D.

All rights reserved.
Published in the United States by Crown Publishers, an imprint of the
Crown Publishing Group, a division of Random House, Inc., New York.
www.crownpublishing.com

CROWN and the Crown colophon are registered trademarks of
Random House, Inc.

Library of Congress Cataloging-in-Publication Data
Perry, Steve, school principal.
Push has come to shove : getting our kids the education they deserve,
even if it means picking a fight / Steve Perry.
p. cm.
Summary: "a guide to saving America's schools"—Provided by publisher.
1. School improvement programs—United States.   I. Title.
LB2822.82.P47 2011
371.2'07—dc22   2011010504

ISBN 978-0-307-72031-3
eISBN 978-0-307-72033-7

Printed in the United States of America

BOOK DESIGN BY GRETCHEN ACHILLES
JACKET DESIGN BY JEAN TRAINA

10 9 8 7 6 5 4 3 2 1

FIRST EDITION

*To all the families and children who have
allowed me to play a role in their lives.*

Contents

PUSH HAS COME TO SHOVE

Introduction

MY WIFE REMINDED me recently that, when we first met back in Philly, I'd promised her an exciting life. I was just talking big. I was twenty-four years old, broke, and so skinny that my shoulder bones made it look like I'd left my shirts on the hanger for too long. All I had was a promise.

An exciting life? Come on. I was just trying to sound cool. I had no idea what an *exciting* life would look like seventeen years ago. I do now.

Push Has Come to Shove is a story about what happens when you fall in love. There's no science or logic to falling in love. If there were, either love would be more predictable or its impact would be less powerful.

I'm often referred to as a "tough love" principal. Yeah, that's true. I'm in love. And I can confirm that *all* love is tough.

When I was younger, I never dreamed of being a principal, never interviewed for the job—but then this principal's life called me. It was a blind date. I was a social worker, a community college adjunct professor, and the director of a pre-collegiate program. I was pleased, doing good work—but not in *love*. I still felt unfulfilled. I knew there was something else out there for me. I knew that there was a life in education—but I didn't know what it was. When she called in 2002, I was ready.

The day I declared that I wanted to start a school was the day that the fighting began. This book is so deeply personal because helping you to educate your kids desperately matters to me.

Solutions greet you throughout the book. This is the result of my being a member of a dedicated, groundbreaking team of educators. We've learned a lot from our success, which makes it possible to share answers to issues that you may have believed to be intractable. The solutions we uncovered from our battles with parents, politicians, pontificators, and bureaucrats will help you be a better parent. They could also improve your kids' school.

My team and I have both lost and found ourselves while building the Capital Preparatory Magnet School in Hartford, Connecticut. Today we're a family of educators where once we used to be coworkers. The journey from colleagues to family has brought great insight. Each section of this book introduces you to the challenges we encountered and how we beat them to become one of America's most successful schools.

I want education to make sense to you, even the things that are designed to be complicated. I want to give parents like you the information that my single mom could've used. I've spelled out those "frequently asked questions" that I get from caring parents, but more important, I've tried to offer practical, real-world solutions. (And though this book is mostly for you parents, I also hope plenty of teachers and my fellow principals will read it, because I've tucked in some helpful pointers for them, too.)

I hope that sharing the love I've found in helping children will—at the least—help you to help your own children. Perhaps it will even inspire you to get further involved in the struggle— and yes, it's a *daily* struggle—to help other children.

Push has definitely come to shove. I've taken all that I can take. America's children deserve better and we can give it to them.

For me, answering that call to start a school and commit to the tough love of marriage delivered the grown-up version of an exciting life and gave birth to my life's purpose.

PART ONE

Inspiration

The Promise

THERE WERE TWO boys who'd grown up together—both poor, both living in public housing, both Black and both with big, really big dreams. Both were athletes—football was their game. They weren't related, though they spent some part of every day together. They rode bikes, played door-knob-ditch together, convinced the girls to hide-and-go-get together, cheated on tests together, stole from convenience stores together, and grew—together. They weren't related, but these two boys were brothers.

High school brought change for each of them. One took to the streets, selling drugs—the other didn't. It wasn't that the boy who didn't sell drugs *loved* school; he just didn't see any future in the sale of drugs. These two young men still spent almost every single day together until they graduated high school. They still played sports together, still convinced the girls together, but they weren't stealing together. Knocking on doors stopped making sense before high school came to a close.

The drug dealer stayed behind and continued selling. The other kid went to college. At each break, they got together, two friends—brothers—living very different lives, still dreaming big, together, separately.

When they'd connect, they'd break into a familiar dialogue:

"Yo, college boy, you need some money?" the drug dealer

would ask. His thinly veiled ribbing aside, the drug dealer was genuinely concerned about his college friend. He didn't know how much college cost, but he knew that just months before, both were poor. The college boy's father was in prison, and his mom was still living in the projects. The drug dealer lived with both of his parents.

The college boy's response was always the same: "Even if I did, I wouldn't take it from *you*. . . ." Then he'd dutifully return the volley. "You still selling that mess?" he'd jab, his words sounding more concerned than judgmental.

The drug dealer's response was equally predictable. "You just stay in college and become a lawyer," he said, laughing. "I might need one someday."

"Stop selling that mess," the college boy would warn, "and you won't *need* one."

This—this teasing—is how young men talk. It's how they show affection, check in on a friend who is living a different life, making his own way, dreaming his own dream.

YEARS PASSED, AND this performance was repeated every Thanksgiving, Christmas, Easter, and summer break. The drug dealer was making his way in his world, and the college kid was making his. Both were successful, standouts, racing together to validate their separate paths, hoping to meet again, at the top.

Then, four years and too many breaks to count later, the poverty, stress, and rising cost of education finally caught up to the college kid. He was a senior, and, with one semester left, he was out of money and time. His single mother and his father, recently paroled from prison, couldn't help. His success on campus had put him on the dean's list but didn't earn him out of his circumstances. So, in anticipation of the fate promised in all the letters that he'd intercepted from the bursar's office, the college boy packed for his final Christmas break.

With his car filled to the windows, he pulled up to his old neighborhood, where his friend was working. The drug dealer made his way over to the college boy, ready to launch into his part, "Yo, college boy. . . ."

"Not today" popped back. When men, even young men, see a friend, another young man, a brother in trouble, they know better than to ask a bunch of questions, delve into how he's *feeling*, make him talk. The exchanges are as uncomfortable for the listener as they are for the one being questioned. Men, even men in training, fall back, say little, and try to get to the end of the conversation as soon as possible with as little outward emotion as possible. When they're hurt, the last thing they want to do is talk. The drug dealer knew this rule of engagement. Just looking at the overstuffed Hyundai and his brother's somber face told him something was up.

Had poverty finally conquered him? Unprompted: "How much do you need?"

Unable to let his pride cut off the discussion, the college boy looked down at the cold December ground and said nothing. In the silence, the winds of reality blew, carrying a respect for space, circumstance, and dignity. After what felt like a season, the college boy heaved what he thought would be an uncatchable ball: "Thirty-five hundred bucks!"

His friend thought about it for a moment. "Yo, can I get it to you on Sunday?" The offer, though unexpected and greatly appreciated, provoked nothing more than silence. Men, even young men, even when they are hurting, don't have much to say.

"I'm good," the college boy said, unconvincingly. The drug dealer shot his friend a questioning glance; the college boy answered with a nod and an awkward exit. "It's cold as hell out here. I'm heading in."

The college boy's mom didn't know that he couldn't return to college after the Christmas break. The young man planned to wait until after the holidays, hoping to either avoid telling her or, better still, to find a last-ditch solution.

This visit was the weekend before exams. Monday morning, he returned to school and began his final packing. All that was left in his bedroom were posters of SUCCESS and great Black leaders such as Martin Luther King Jr. and Malcolm X. As the college boy peeled the gooey Malcolm X poster off the wall, he stopped and said, "To *hell* with this." He pivoted and stormed out of his room, through campus, headed to the college president's office. When he got there, he was greeted by a polite and persistent secretary. Within seconds, his anger and hurt had elevated the situation to a threat of security being called.

Hearing the commotion, and recognizing the student, the president stepped out and intervened. Seeing his visitor, a campus leader, now in a full froth, complete with reddened eyes and balled fists, the president asked the student to come into his office.

"I'm broke," the student wasted no time in saying. "I've been broke since I was born and it's just gotten worse since I came here.

I did everything y'all asked and I'm still broke and now *I* gotta go home. Not the fools who drink from Monday to Monday. *Me*."

The president listened as the young man fought back rage, hurt, and tears. Then he asked, "How much do you need?"

Without a breath: "Thirty-five hundred."

Convinced that this old White guy was playing him, the student grew truly agitated when the president said, "I can help— under one condition."

"Look," the young man said, "I've just left all this money in my drug dealer friend's pocket. What could *you* possibly ask me to do that I will say no to?"

As I said, "I can give you the money under one condition . . ."

"Anything."

"That you use it to give kids like you a chance."

THE COLLEGE BOY graduated, went on to an Ivy League graduate school, managed a homeless shelter, ran for state representative, started the Capital Preparatory Magnet School, and wrote five books, including the one you hold in your hands. . . .

I made a promise to President Robert Carothers and I've spent my life making good on that promise. Education and an educator saved my life; now I must do the same. I started Capital Prep, tour the country giving speeches, and have written this book because I know that America has failed to develop a successful public school system that can be replicated across racial and class lines. This book—and the life that I'm living—explain why we've failed and how we can be successful.

The Push

I DIDN'T START this fight, but I'm damn sure gonna finish it. Back in 2001, I got dragged into the battle by an innocent-sounding question. When Ms. Saunders asked me, "Why do only rich kids get good schools?" I didn't have a good answer.

Ms. Saunders was one of the parents in a pre-collegiate program for low-income students that I'd started and had been running since 1998. Her question called me out and pushed me into a fight from which I couldn't turn back. I didn't get in it thinking that I *could* win. But she made me feel I *had* to.

Urban schools are America's canary. The shafts are dangerous. Traveling them will cost more than money. The 'hood's academic discord and dysfunction don't end at the city limits nor do they dissipate with a lightening of the students' hue. Like drugs, divorce, and out-of-wedlock births, the issues surrounding America's need to offer quality education are easiest to see in urban communities. There the issues are so pronounced that they're impossible to avoid.

Yet the bucolic bends and tree-lined streets of our affluent suburbs hide a very ugly truth. *All* America's children are being offered an un-American education.

Ms. Saunders had dreams, but dreams don't pay the bills. She was haunted by the pursuit of a good education for her child. She was fed up because traditional neighborhood schools—urban or suburban—aren't working for anybody. Was she excessive, hypersensitive, a conspiracy theorist? Yup—all three. She was pugnacious on a good day, rude on a bad one. However, even a stopped clock is right twice a day. It happened to be her time.

Ms. Saunders had gone to great lengths to send her teenage daughter, Kayla, to nearby Windsor High School in a middle-class suburb. But therein lay the problem. Kayla's suburban school was not designed to send all of its students to college. Windsor High is an example of what is happening all over the country in suburban schools. It presents a pretty façade, offering parents false confidence. The root of that false sense of confidence can be found in one word: *proficient*.

Each school is like a car dealership. The dealership knows the rules better than you. No matter how much research you do before you go into the showroom, if the salesman is a shady individual, you are going to walk out with an expensive, unsolvable problem. Seminar, advanced placement (AP), honors, college prep, and basic—the most common academic tracks—ensure that most of the kids in the school will not be ready for college. How would you know this? You wouldn't. It's damn near impossible to figure out, even when you're an educator yourself.

To convince the community that the schools are in fact working, states and districts often focus on students' performance being "proficient." The problem is that to be categorized as "proficient" is to be performing *below grade level*.

Each state's standardized tests are typically scored on a scale from 1 to 5: 1 is "below basic"; 2 is "basic"; 3 is "proficient"; 4 is "at goal"; 5 is "at or above goal." Lauding proficiency is nothing short of accepting mediocrity. It essentially means that a tenth-grader who is proficient in writing is *almost* writing on the tenth-grade level. If we care about truly educating our kids, only performance "at goal" can matter.

But since proficiency is what's reported, Ms. Saunders and the other suburban parents had reason to feel pretty good. In 2010, for instance, almost 90 percent of the White students were proficient in math, reading, writing, and science in Windsor. A slightly closer look would reveal that less than 60 percent of these same White students were at goal in math, science, reading, and writing. That's a stunning statistic when you consider it: according to the 2009 Connecticut Academic Performance Test, fully *60 percent* of the White students at this supposedly "high-performing" suburban high school failed to do science at grade level.

As the founder and director of the Connecticut Collegiate Awareness and Preparation Program—or ConnCAP—I'd spent five years working with teachers in the communities of Hartford, Windsor, East Hartford, and Bloomfield, fighting for the kids that didn't have Ms. Saunders as a mom. I fought to make teachers stay after school with our kids for extra help, respect our kids in class, and expect more for these low-income students.

Ms. Saunders had a hunch and a fighter's spirit. She knew that something was wrong with the way her daughter was being educated, but she did not know how much she was kept in the dark, or what remedies she could take to get her daughter on a track toward academic success.

What Ms. Saunders needed was a school she could afford and that was designed to send every single kid to college. But that was going to be a heavyweight bout.

Until then, I'd been slapboxing. All I was doing was moving kids from one class to another, looking for the best teachers in poorly designed and ineffective schools. I wasn't solving the problem. I was shifting chairs on the deck of the *Titanic,* giving students a better view of a sinking ship.

"Well," Ms. Saunders asked, "why can't this program become its own school?"

That wasn't the question anymore: it was the *answer.*

Over those years at ConnCAP, I'd met some amazing educators in failing schools. We'd all talked about doing something, but we didn't know what.

These teachers, all with résumés from various public schools, had already become outcasts and disenchanted. What none of us ever really considered was starting our own school. Yeah, we would vaguely talk about it, but nobody was eager to leave their job and give up tenure to support this silly-ass idea of creating our own public school from scratch.

Ms. Saunders's question changed all that. She needed an answer. When she hit me with that question, I went from being a spectator, enjoying a good run as the director of a successful non-profit, to a pissed-off pugilist ready for an all-out brawl.

Starting a school gave all of us hope, but be clear: we had more ambition than good sense. None of us had ever even met anyone who'd started a public school. Every school we'd ever seen had always *been* there—usually decades before we were even born.

Ambitious? Hell, yeah. We'd made our minds up that we were going to change education as we knew it. Okay, some of us had. Most everybody else was running from a burning building to one that reeked of gas.

Push had come to shove. We'd all seen too much to turn another cheek. We'd run out of cheeks.

This book is about what happens next. It's the story about one group of educators' vision. *Push Has Come to Shove* is about deciding whether to sit back and do nothing or do something difficult, risky, and seemingly impossible. It's about the process—again, that *daily* struggle—to address Ms. Saunders's simple question.

Push Has Come to Shove and Capital Prep serve the exact same purpose. They each exist to answer parents' endless questions about the struggle to educate and save our nation's children.

PART TWO

Purpose

Why Should You Care?

SO WHY SHOULD you care? Your own kids are going to be just fine, right? They go to good public schools, you help them with their homework every weeknight, and, more important, the "achievement gap" only negatively impacts kids in low-performing urban schools, right? Yeah, okay. Keep believing that.

Even if you're from some of the top-ranked places to live in the USA—Columbia, Maryland; Eden Prairie, Minnesota; Ames, Iowa—you need to be aware of sobering facts about public education in this country. There's very little difference in the way that the best suburban neighborhood schools and the worst urban schools are run. Each feels big and impersonal—most have ten feeder elementary schools funneling into one middle school and then one gigantic-feeling high school.

Kids in suburban schools often complain of feeling like they don't fit in. So what happens? Those kids form cliques. Kids in the 'hood do, too, but we call our cliques gangs. When students—from all socioeconomic backgrounds—start to feel disconnected and severely alienated, these groups take on antisocial behavior. In the 'hood, it takes the form of a drive-by. In the suburbs, it becomes Columbine. A kid from either the 'hood or the 'burbs who isn't a standout athlete or a budding rock star gets stuck with that "uncool" label. And a label can become unshakable. As the years go by, these kids feel more and more like social outcasts and, for them, the experience of going to school becomes hellish.

We often hear that the United States is losing the educational race to countries like Korea and Finland. But let's be real: many Americans hear those rankings and think, *So what?* We may buy millions of Samsung and Nokia products, but neither of these countries is big enough to present a real threat to our economy— after all, we're the United States of America! But consider China. We can't deny that China is a real economic threat, right? And guess what? In 2009, the very first year that China participated in the PISA—the Program for International Student Assessment, which analyzes the performance of fifteen-year-olds from some sixty-five national school systems—students from Shanghai blew away all the experts by outscoring everyone in reading as well as in math and science.

But we don't even need to look at how the United States ranks against other nations to see how dysfunctional our public school system has become. Our *own* colleges tell us that our *own* students can't do college work. A 2008 report titled *Diploma to Nowhere,* conducted by the advocacy group Strong American Schools, "conservatively" estimated that 43 percent of students at two-year colleges and almost 30 percent of students enrolled in four-year public institutions nationwide had taken a remedial course. The cost of that remediation? An annual $2.5 billion. To essentially *repeat* what they were supposed to have learned in high school!

Don't kid yourself that these remedial course takers are the lowest-achieving among our college students. The study reported that 80 percent of remedial students surveyed had maintained at least a 3.0 grade point average during high school. "We looked at race, ethnicity, and socioeconomic backgrounds," said Rachel Bird, a senior policy analyst for Strong American Schools. "The problem exists across the board. Remediation affects low-income to middle-income to high-income students." Bob Wise, the former West Virginia governor and head of the Alliance for Excellent Education, said that he's seen students at the top of their class—even valedictorians—go on to take remedial courses in college.

Yes, a shamefully high number of college and university freshmen have to take remedial noncredit college courses upon entering. These numbers are too big to represent poor minority students—too few go to college to impact the numbers so significantly. Suburban students from good homes, good communities, and supposedly good schools are coming into college unprepared to write, read, research, or *think* on a college level.

This should frighten the hell out of us. These kids are among the brightest of our young people—the ones who've actually made it to an American college campus. If they can't do college-level work, then what does that say about the tens of millions who never make it past high school? The costs are enormous, both in the financial outlay to the K–12 schools and colleges and in the loss of income that would have come to those who were admitted to college but couldn't complete a degree.

THERE ARE A multitude of reasons why our schools fall woefully short on the world stage. One factor often cited is that we have this so-called Black/White achievement gap. As long as there are

American groups—underprivileged subcultures, some would call them—doing demonstrably worse than the White kids in the suburbs, it's easy for White parents to feel good about themselves. It's easy to live in a bubble of false confidence. You'll actually hear people say things like, *Well, if we could factor out the poor schools, all those miserable "inner-city" scores, the U.S. would be on par with those other developed countries.* What are they smoking? This isn't some deli counter where you can shave off the inedible ends of the ham. You cannot lop off these tens of millions of underperforming students and then try to redo the math. News flash: even if you *tried* some funky recalculations, the U.S. still wouldn't be on top. In fact, Finland's bottom 10 percent is better than our *top* 10 percent. So much for that silly-ass *theory.* . . .

Our colleges and employers can't say it loudly enough: we're sending them graduates who are completely unprepared. I often meet professors who are fed up. They want to teach university and college students. They want to teach university- and college-*level* concepts—not "refresher" courses in basic composition.

Now, we do have a model of what works for us. This may surprise you, but there is a great similarity between successful urban charter and magnet schools and successful private schools. Both have high expectations, talented instructors and leaders, compelling curricula, and an advisory system that makes all students feel like they are cared for. The problem is that these schools educate such a small proportion of America's children as to not be much of a factor in our country's overall performance.

Face the facts—we've got to fix *all* our schools. There's no other choice. Most of America's kids go to public schools that add no value to their academic capacity. Said differently, if your children come into the seventh grade *barely* able to read, the only direction they'll move is downward. American parents are spending billions annually, expecting that their kids will go to school to eventually—miraculously—become better educated. The sad truth is that American students perform *worse* the longer they stay in our public schools, according to the most recent PSA data.

Yes, *worse*.

America's fourth-graders score in the top 25 percent of industrialized nations on the PISA exam. By the time they reach high school, America's public school students—not just the poor, minority students, mind you, but *all* American high school students—have fallen to the bottom quartile among all industrialized nations.

According to the 2009 McKinsey report on education, "If the United States had in recent years closed the gap between its educational achievement levels and those of better-performing nations such as Finland and Korea, GDP in 2008 could have been $1.3 trillion to $2.3 trillion higher. This represents 9 to 16 percent of GDP."*

Note—this report *ain't sayin'* "If Black kids, Hispanic kids, or kids from public housing projects performed better, then the country will move up the economic ladder." Rather, it's saying that if the country as a whole performed better academically, we would have brought in enough money to erase much of the

....

* *The Economic Impact of the Achievement Gap in America's Schools: Summary of Findings* (McKinsey & Company, April 2009), 5, http://www.mckinsey.com/app_media/images/ page_images/offices/socialsector/pdf/achievement_gap_report.pdf.

nation's deficit. *Damn.* In some important respects, then, the American education crisis is the American *economic* crisis. We all need to own it and will suffer from it until we fix it.

You don't have to care—that is your choice—but you will *pay* for it.

Sue 'Em!

SUE YOUR SCHOOL district for damages. We've done the whole civil rights bit—marching, writing letters, organizing parents' groups—while conditions in American schools have steadily deteriorated.

So why file a lawsuit? Because there are direct and measurable damages that can be assessed to schools that fail to educate kids to fully participate in postsecondary education or the economy.

We spend as much as 80 percent of our collective property taxes on education. We've got one simple expectation: that the schools will train children to read, write, and compute at the level necessary to go to college or to go directly into the economy.

A high school diploma is, in effect, a contract that grants the recipient "all rights and privileges" due to a person who has met the requirements as set forth by the state, city, and district. When I hand one to a student and shake his hand, I'm confirming that he has completed the requirements. I'm declaring to the community that this young person may commence the next phase of his life, whether it be professional or further education. It's that literal. It's that *legal,* too.

As a high school principal, I'm making my own binding agreement, confirming that each hand that I shake, each diploma I bestow, belongs to a student who can read, write, and compute on a level that is consistent with a person who wants either to go to college or to start working. Graduation is more than a ceremony. It's a public declaration that my staff, my teachers, and I have done our jobs to educate. It's my job—not the job of the student, his parents, politicians, society, or anybody else—to make sure my teachers teach him, to make sure he can read, write, and compute at a level that will allow him to go to college or work. *Only* after the student has demonstrated that he can meet the requirements am I authorized to present him with a high school diploma.

Parents, you have every reason to presume that when you send your children to a public school, we are teaching them what the state, district, and school deem to be in line with what colleges and the economy require. When we don't, you have a case for a breach of contract and damages.

Physicians of every type have malpractice insurance for the (hopefully unlikely) time in a career when science and nature don't jibe and a patient gets hurt. Attorneys who don't appropriately represent a client can be disbarred. Who pays—who's held accountable—when a kid has to take remedial classes in his freshman year of college because he can't read or write on a college level?

Nobody blames patients for botched surgery. Nobody blames defendants burdened with an inept attorney. Enron's retiring employees were not scapegoated when their bosses pillaged their pension funds. Yet the current rationale in public education is that it is a fourth-grader's fault for reading below level.

If we educators want to be respected and remunerated like the highest-paid professionals, then we have to accept the same

high-stakes responsibility. A doctor can't use some weak excuse—*the patient was sick when she got here*—to explain why he
prescribed the wrong meds. Of course, the patient was sick; that's
why she came to see a doctor! Educators, however, can use this
lame-ass excuse and get away with not educating our students.

When we say that a kid couldn't read when we got him, it absolves us of the responsibility for curing his educational illness.
Throw socioeconomic factors like race, class, and multigenera-
tional poverty into the equation and we can leave the kid as illiterate and dysfunctional as we found him and then shout that it's
not our fault. Let a physician try this and see how quickly she's
banished from the profession.

Even bike messengers can't fail at a rate comparable to teachers and principals. Nor can cab drivers, chefs, or hairdressers.
Would you use a delivery service or a hair salon if it posted a 50
percent failure rate? No other group in the economy, from professionals to blue-collar workers, stays employed with failure rates
as high as America's educators.

Educators get away with failing to teach our kids to state and
local standards by falling back on the same old defense: *I tried.
I really tried.* As long as we can say—not *prove*—that we tried,
we can hand out diplomas to kids who can't even read them and
keep on shouting that it's not our fault.

Can you imagine a pilot trying something so ludicrous with
the FAA? Claiming, before a flight, that he would *try* to land the
airliner safely? Can you imagine a carpet cleaner leaving your car-
pets filthy and using as his excuse, "I tried." Yeah, you'll recommend this guy to your friends: "The rugs still look nasty but, man,
does he try!" It sounds crazy because it *is* crazy.

Failure to educate children is inhumane and should become a criminal offense punishable by, at the very least, a loss of license, or at most, prison. Sound over the top? Well, think about the standard that society holds parents to. When a parent fails to send just one school-age child to school, it's considered "educational neglect," a crime punishable by fines and prison. When a school categorically fails to educate thousands of children, educators shrug and say, "We *tried*."

The loss of one kid is a tragedy. The loss of thousands of kids is a statistic. It's unconscionable to believe that one uneducated parent is more culpable for withholding education than the dozens upon dozens of educators that a child will encounter during her twelve years in school. The reason we're able to blame parents is because educators have well-funded union lawyers and all you have is your parental guilt.

The time has come for a new day in the pursuit of educational equity. Historically, the civil courts were a battleground for the rights of the disenfranchised. The time has come for a new generation of complainants to again use the civil courts. However, this time, a different strategy is needed. End the fights over mandated busing. Curtail the discussion regarding magnets and charters. Today, educational "civil rights workers" must sue for damages.

This isn't some theoretical game. We can talk dollars and cents. We can calculate lost wages and earning potential. According to a recent U.S. Census Bureau report titled *The Big Payoff: Educational Attainment and Synthetic Estimates of Work-Life,* people with bachelor's degrees earn nearly $1 million more over the course of their careers than those without. And those with master's degrees and doctorates earn millions more over the course of their careers:

Bachelor's degree—Holders of bachelor's degrees can expect to earn $900,000 more than a high school graduate over the course of their career.

Master's degree—Holders of master's degrees can expect to earn $1.3 million more than a high school graduate.

Doctoral degree—Holders of doctoral degrees can expect to earn $2.2 million more than a high school graduate.

Professional degree—Those with other professional degrees can expect to earn $3.2 million more than a high school graduate.*

And we can also put a dollar value on the impact that poverty has on health, happiness, and the overall well-being of the family. This number could be calculated and assessed against every district. Then we will begin to see justice in public education for students. Nothing—not race, marital status of parents, income, or education—has a greater impact on children's life prospects than their level of education. Most crucial is what is learned in those years from pre-kindergarten to twelfth grade.

It doesn't matter that there are some good teachers and administrators in these raggedy-ass schools. The results are frighteningly consistent and lackluster. Teachers and principals in the most dysfunctional school systems fail more kids than they educate. We—and I speak collectively of my fraternity and sorority of educators—play a vital role in the destruction of more lives

---

*The Big Payoff: Educational Attainment and Synthetic Estimates of Work-Life (U.S. Census Bureau, July 2002), http://www.census.gov/prod/2002pubs/p23-210.pdf).

than we save. Paying us when we fail is pissing good tax dollars down the drain. Keeping us employed after repeated failure is simply criminal. Sure, we are nice people, but there's no other way of saying it—many of us suck at our jobs.

The time has come for the civil and criminal justice system to hold us accountable for our failings.

EDUCATION PAYS

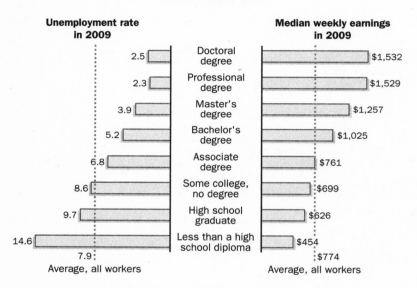

Source: Bureau of Labor Statistics, Current Population Survey

We can monetize the damages suffered by children who have been the victims of "educational malpractice"— call an attorney; organize and file a class action lawsuit against your local school district.

E-Organize

THE LAST THING a superintendent wants to see is a group of well-organized, hi-tech parents. His stomach churns when his inbox fills with e-mails from regular folks who have the wherewithal to use technology to organize other parents.

Understand—board meetings are *old*-school. Nothing meaningful gets decided at them. By the time public school board meetings are scheduled, there have been weeks, perhaps months, of private meetings during which every issue was discussed and divvied up among the power brokers. So you go to the board meeting, wait to read your speech, get all hyped, and then the next person reads hers and the next reads his, and on and on until the public session is done. Yep, that was a productive evening. . . .

The superintendent and the board have got a surefire answer for your emotional outbursts at the board of ed meetings. *Ma'am, meet Police Officer Norello.* They're well prepared for a bunch of parents publicly losing their composure, showing righteous indignation. Here's what they're *not* ready for. They're not prepared for you and the other parents to inundate the board members *before* the meetings, when the real decisions are being made as to how money will be allocated. They aren't ready for "e-organized"

parents who, one after another, deluge them with research, statistics, and strategies to improve your school.

As I said, the board meetings are little more than a kind of
stage show, a public reading of what has already been decided. It's
a place where the crazies filibuster while the board members sit
back smirking, text their friends, complete their own work, and
otherwise pay no attention to the raw emotion on display before
them.

However, when you take your fight to the Internet, the discussion is elevated and your kids will benefit.

Start with the principal. Conversations are cool, phone calls
are fine, but you need a *record* of what was said to and by whom.
E-mails are critical at work, right? Well, consider that improving
your child's school is this person's job. It's time for you to start
interacting with the school as if it is *your* job, too. If you don't get
what you want from the principal, take it to the central office.
Trust me—all they have is time. Just don't spin your wheels too
long dealing with the central office. The suits there have fancy job
titles, but, in reality, they have no juice. Use them to set up a time
to meet with the superintendent.

Now this is the key: Don't meet with the super *too* soon. Send
a few e-mails, let your voices be heard, and then keep him guess-
ing. One of the benefits of the Internet is that it conceals how
many of you there are. When you and three other parents go to
a board meeting, you are just that—four parents. But when four
parents *e-mail* in concert, it can seem like a *movement*. And in a
matter of days, it can become a real movement. We all know that
e-mail spreads like wildfire. No district is equipped to combat

e-organized parents. This strategy has toppled governments in the Middle East. It'll work with a superintendent, too.

Don't be discouraged if you're initially ignored or get a glib e-mail from an ineffectual administrator. This is just the first step. Be persistent. Follow up. Send still more e-mails and you'll eventually get the result you want—a face-to-face meeting.

No educators should be safe from your searing and thoughtful assessment of your children's education. The board meeting is the theater, but again, no real decisions get made there.

Confront the teachers', custodians', secretaries', and administrators' unions and associations using the same methods. They are even less equipped to combat your e-mail campaign. The private discussions between unions and the board are where all the decisions that impact your kids' school are made. The budget that you just learned about was actually drawn up two *years* earlier during negotiations between the unions and the board.

PARENTS, YOU MUST e-organize to get a seat at the negotiation table. This is where you will be able to ask the questions that matter to the people who will decide. In these meetings, union and board attorneys take almost all of your tax dollars and assign them as they see fit. Hundreds of millions of dollars will be assigned within weeks for the next two years and you'll go to a board meeting with speech in hand.

Yes, you *can* change the system. Yes, you can use the Internet better than Barack Obama to start a campaign for your freedom from the tyranny of raggedy-ass schools. Twitter and Facebook it. YouTube, blog, text, and e-mail your desires to gain access to a good American education. You deserve it. Every *single one of you* deserves it.

Past generations had to march for miles, had to crowd segregated lunch counters, had to sit cross-legged and defenseless while police dogs barked in their faces, fire hoses blasted, and rocks were thrown. You can bring your school district to its knees from your PC or Mac. You are the e-warriors. Log on and shut 'em down.

PART THREE

School

What Makes a Good Teacher?

EVERYBODY KNOWS a good teacher when they see one. No principal's certification is needed. No framed awards or accolades. Nothing but some good ol' common sense. Good teachers make us feel smart. They make the impossible seem possible. We want them to tell us how to do *anything*, because we know that when they're done, we'll be better at something that matters.

Good teachers are *born*, not made. There's just something about them—some mysterious character trait—that they've had all their lives. Teaching is an art, a God-given talent, like singing, painting, and writing. Sure, a bad singer can learn to hit fewer off-key notes in the shower, an average weekend painter can get his blotches to look like a still life. But nobody—not even a *great* teacher—can create a good teacher.

Teachers teach all of the time. Take a moment and watch them at a cookout. Without prompting, they'll organize the children into teams, call them in from tag, get them in to wash their hands, and then line them up from biggest to smallest to pass out paper plates and plastic cutlery, waiting patiently for their turn in the burger line while the rest of us watch in amazement.

When the rest of us sit eating, teachers' minds are always at work, trying to figure another way to teach sixth-graders to read. In their free time, they coach. In their downtime, they teach Hebrew at the local Jewish Community Center. Between classes, they turn their duty-free lunch into a brown-bag problem-solving session. They live for the adrenaline rush that comes when a bad-ass kid looks up from the back of the room and says, out of turn and without raising his hand, "Miss, I get it." A good teacher chases those fleeting feelings like a junkie. This isn't the life he chose. It's the life that chose him.

Most parents know intuitively that smart teachers are better teachers. As far back as 1998, the Education Trust found that "the most significant factor in student achievement [is] the teacher." This is why, for decades, parents have sought to get their kids in the *good* teacher's class. The challenge facing you, as parents, is clear: knowing who the good teachers are. If you are not familiar with the school, of course, you don't have insight into how good your son's teacher is until he's already enrolled in her class. You need to know if your child's teacher is effective before he ever sets foot in that class.

When I was a graduate student in Philadelphia, I interned at an ugly school with a pretty name. In 1993, Strawberry Mansion High School was a mess—dangerous, dark, and depressing. Daily I wondered how the kids could get up to go through the hell of some of the nearby neighborhoods to come to a place that felt more dangerous and disorganized than many prisons I have visited. Each day I felt like I was climbing a wet glass wall—I got no traction.

The kids at Mansion were the same as any other kids I'd worked with. Their issues ran the gamut from petty teenage nonsense to some real foul adult abuse. It's what you come to expect when working in these settings. Class after class at the Penn School of Social Work warned us of the perils of adolescence and poverty.

My responsibility was to work with the kids who were "at risk." Funny, actually, because everybody in the whole school was "at risk." Basketball games had to be played immediately after school because night games had a nasty tendency to become bench-clearing melees. My internship supervisor told us to be out of the school immediately after the day ended at 2:00 p.m. I listened.

My kids were the Sweat Hogs. We'd do something called "family group"—some days it felt more like a group therapy session from *One Flew over the Cuckoo's Nest*. One of the kids who had the greatest impact on me was named Kevin. He was a fourteen-year-old freshman who couldn't read a stop sign. No, that's not hyperbole. The boy could not read S-T-O-P. Kevin knew that he couldn't read. But I didn't. I wanted to believe he was smarter than he acted. I refused to believe a kid his age could be wholly illiterate. To prove to him that he was smart and could read, I wrote the word *stop* on a Post-it. He stuttered, stammered, stumbled, and stuttered some more. Kevin was right. He couldn't read. But it turned out that I was right, too. He was much smarter than he looked.

For all my challenges with the "at risk" kids, I had no idea that the greatest challenge I'd confront would be the adults. The teachers and administration at Strawberry Mansion were a mess. I was twenty-three and trying to fit in. Like so many inspired young people seeking the opportunity to make a difference in schools, I met the reality of education's establishment, the gatekeepers, in the ubiquitous teachers' lounge.

Some twenty years later, I have since seen this in too many teachers' lounges at too many schools to mention. I discovered it at Strawberry Mansion and I've encountered it at every school I've worked in since. Most folks get caught up on school gossip, complain about their jobs, brag about their children, and plan their break—typical employee lounge chatter. There is, however, a much darker side.

I was nauseated to see firsthand how often the teachers at Strawberry Mansion *annihilated* the kids in the teachers' lounge. Be clear—no one expects teachers to be saints; there are kids that can be difficult, if not downright impossible, to like. A small number of students are obnoxious brats; the vast majority are just caught up in the hormonal mayhem of being kids. Professionals quickly learn to let most of the obnoxious remarks roll off their backs. Still, too many of the teachers at schools like Mansion become jaded, complacent, and comfortable crossing the line. When their students acted out in childish ways, they didn't bother to mask their grown-up disdain. Though it was only a few teachers regularly making fun of students' clothes, classroom inadequacies, uneducated parents—or more often than not, the lack thereof—their colleagues all too often remained silent.

It didn't take long for me to stop going to the teachers' lounge. I ate lunch alone or not at all. I didn't need friends *that* bad.

Kids see everything. Even the ones who aren't "book smart" can possess deep reserves of emotional intelligence. They'd come in to my dank office and tell me what was up among the staff—which teachers hated each other, which ones were dating on the sly. But Kevin—sullen, illiterate Kevin—rarely joined the conversation. Alone among my Sweat Hogs, he didn't seem to observe *anything*.

Then, one day during a typically raucous afternoon of "family group," Kev's voice popped out of the chatter.

"Mr. Steve," he said. "How could these teachers teach us when they don't even *like* us?"

Kevin? We were all stunned. It was like that Juicy Fruit moment in *Cuckoo's Nest* when Big Chief speaks for the first time and we realize that he's been playacting as a mentally challenged mute to survive the brutality of the psychiatric institution. Kevin had never spoken before in group, but this question was both brave and insightful. He put it out there. The other kids quickly jumped into the mix. They became animated as they each shared stories of offhanded and painful statements that teachers had made. They told me about having their homework thrown into the trash can, being made to read aloud when the teacher knew full well that they couldn't, and otherwise being put on "front street" in class by adults who they were told to respect. My jaw dropped as the kids unloaded: Kevin's observation had taken over my group and, in an instant, changed my life forever. . . .

I walked home that night, still stunned and confused: How in the hell did he know? How did he figure out that my colleagues really didn't like him? Here was a kid all the gossips in the teachers' lounge considered "dumb as a bag of rocks," but Kevin was smart enough to see through their professional façade. He knew that these teachers couldn't spend a forty-five-minute free period dogging kids out in the lounge, open the door, walk across the hall, put on a smiling mask, and teach them how to read, write, and live.

For all the lectures and seminars I was doing in grad school, yes, it was Kevin who taught me what it takes to be a great teacher. He punctured one of our sessions with that simple question. Kevin knew that he didn't know much. He said little that could be seen as positive. His rare outbursts tended to derail discussions and were attempts to deflect the obvious limits that he dragged through each day.

But Kevin caught their asses. He nailed their hypocrisy. How the *hell* could they teach him when they didn't even *like* him?

A GOOD TEACHER must love children. She must love them enough to get angry when the child comes to class and acts up, doesn't do his homework, or otherwise falls short of his potential. A good teacher must care because kids will do nothing for people who they know don't like them and everything for people who do.

I don't know what happened to Kev. Even before I left Mansion, we'd lost touch. I hate to say it, but he's probably dead today. No young black man could have so little academic ability, so much pent-up fury—be so *damned* aware of it—and survive the streets. Nobody could be so devoid of skill and filled with that much anger and not end up on the other side of a bullet. Man, he was an angry kid, as angry as I've ever known. With so much intuition and so few problem-solving skills, he was ripe to be picked up by a criminal crew who needed a pawn. The streets of Philly are filled with gangsters looking for an angry young soldier like Kev.

For almost twenty years, I've told that Strawberry Mansion

story as if it were mine alone. But then I spoke to Bowling Green State University's School of Teaching and Learning. I asked the undergrads who'd just started their internships if they knew who the bad teachers were, and every hand was raised—followed by voices crying, "Hell, yes!" The same thing happened when I spoke earlier that year in St. Thomas, Virgin Islands. A teachers' union member had approached the mic during Q&A and declared that no evaluation tool existed to determine if a teacher was good. So I turned to a row of middle schoolers and asked, "How many of you know who the bad teachers are in your school?" Their hands shot so high that most of the kids were pulled out of their seats.

Yes, too many educators don't love kids, and the kids know it. When kids feel loved, they will go to war for a teacher. Kevin's question made me step outside of discussions of pedagogy and theory and into the heart of what matters. Kids need to feel connected to the instructor, and when they do, they will work hard to please. This is the real reason why some kids give up on a subject or on school entirely. They don't make the connection that comes from feeling loved. Kevin didn't feel loved and therefore never felt like school was where he was supposed to be. He felt that his crew in the streets had love for him, and so only in the streets did he feel at home.

Malcolm Gladwell, in his best-selling book *Blink,* highlighted a study by psychologist Nalini Ambady. Ambady gave students three ten-second videotapes of a teacher without sound. What she found is that these students had no problem rating the teacher's effectiveness. The researcher then cut the soundless clips to five seconds—the ratings were the same. Gladwell writes that the results were "remarkably consistent even when she showed the students just two seconds of videotape."* Then the researcher compared the snap judgments to those of students who'd had the professors the entire semester. "She found that they were also essentially the same."

Everybody knows who the good teachers are. Too often, parents and noneducational professionals feel they need to possess some special knowledge or skill set that can only come from decades of training and an elaborate evaluation system. That's bull. You don't have to like country music to know if Keith Urban or Faith Hill can sing. Talent is talent. Everybody knows who the most talented and loving teachers are.

Conversely, there's no special training needed to identify a bad teacher. We all know teachers who've been sleepwalking through the same sorry-ass lessons for twenty years. We all know teachers who think that Monday is the worst day of the week and Friday the best.

Both sides of the teacher evaluation issue are wrong. Administrators who make it seem as though it's impossible to identify a good teacher are as bad as the unions who stamp millions of feet in unison every time we start talking about accountability.

If children can identify the artistry of good teachers, then why can't parents and professional educators?

---

*Gladwell, Malcolm. *Blink*. New York: Little, Brown and Company, 2005, p. 12.

How to Find Great Teachers

HIRING QUALITY STAFF is one of the great challenges facing any school. We keep it simple at Capital Prep. Like most successful schools, Capital Prep is composed of a team—teachers, administrators, social workers, and support staff—dedicated to and focused on a single mission. Nothing is more essential to our success story than who we hire and how we do so. There are a few tried-and-true methods that I use to determine if a teacher is going to work out.

Of course, early in my tenure as Capital Prep's principal, I made more than my share of missteps. I've hired some of the nicest, most sincere people who proved to be the worst teachers on earth. They couldn't teach a dog to bark or a fish to swim. The best interview I've ever sat in on was with a young, bilingual Latina with a high grade point average, energetic, smart, and attractive. Yes, she was a world-class interviewee.

She said she wanted to mentor kids who had come from her own underdeveloped community. She said that she'd worked with preteen girls in her free time to improve their self-esteem. She came with incredible recommendations and was willing to start work that day. Unfortunately, that was the last day I was impressed with her. She proved to be both immature and careless. And she was so flighty that she once left a group of girls unattended downtown while she went Christmas shopping.

In the early days, teachers' personal and professional limitations were something that I was oblivious to. My training is in social work and education, not human resources. I wish I could tell you that seven years of interviewing applicants for positions at Capital Prep has brought me all the answers, but I still make my share of mistakes and misjudgments. I'm still stunned by some of the thoughtless and selfish decisions that staff can make. Sure, most teachers are reasonable people, but there have been some horror stories. I've had teachers request "half days" or "flex schedules," knowing damn well that there's no such thing. And I've had teachers resign the day before school starts, knowing that over 120 kids will be left in the hands of a substitute for months or even a full school year. Whatever my blind spots in the hiring department, the reason we haven't been hurt as badly as other schools is because, inevitably, one way or another, the bad seeds are going to be removed from Capital Prep. Knowing that bad behavior will cost you your job is essential to an organization's effectiveness. When losers think that they will get away with murder, they're emboldened; the winners' efforts shrink and ultimately disappear.

Not every teacher, no matter how inspired or talented, is good for every school. They have to fit—and help to advance—the school's mission. Too many of our failing schools are filled with individuals acting individually. Their needs, their desires—and, yes, their *egos*—supersede those of the school. We believe that nobody is bigger than Capital Prep. We believe that Capital Prep is smaller when we act as individuals.

We hire people who want to work at Capital Prep more than anywhere else. If Capital Prep is not the absolute best school for a prospective teacher, he won't connect to our purpose. He won't fight to stay a part of the team. If he feels he can take the job or leave it, then he will likely leave it. Or I'll ask him to leave.

Most folks—especially most teachers—can put together a good-looking résumé. But why on earth do we spend so much time looking at an applicant's CV? No one in his or her right mind is going to forward the name of a reference who'll reveal the down-and-dirty: that an applicant's often a half hour late to work or drives a beat-up Corolla whose upholstery reeks of weed smoke. I don't put much stock in references.

Similarly, almost all teachers have one good lesson in them. Don't put too much effort in evaluating their guest lecture. For that one hour, she was probably the bomb. But can she do it week in and week out? New teachers will always look bad when compared to a seasoned veteran, so don't overvalue a candidate's experience.

So many prospective teachers come in with those huge, beautifully prepared portfolios that their professors told them would be so important. Who's giving them advice on getting a job in a high school? A college professor who's never worked in one. I never look at these things. My academic dean, Mr. Beganski, is even tougher. He'll tell candidates he doesn't give a damn about their portfolios. The point is, if they can't deal with *us*, then the kids are going to break them. We want to see them thinking on their feet. We want to see them deal with pressure because this is what twenty-four kids are going to give them every day.

EACH SCHOOL HAS its own process of hiring staff. No one style is guaranteed to work better than the others. The one that works for your local school is the one that works best. I've been involved with some hiring processes that went on for days. They included staff from throughout the school, students and parents, writing samples, and psychological tests. In a different approach, a small group of faculty asks everyone the same questions, scoring the responses. Other schools hire based on a single one-on-one interview between the candidate and the principal. We've tried them all. The hiring process that works best for us involves my dean and I sitting down and getting to know candidates who are pre-screened—recommended by people we trust.

We start by telling them that Capital Prep will be the hardest assignment they're likely ever going to take on in their teaching careers. We say that we're going to work the hell out of them—then we're going to ask for more. We tell them that we hate to lose at anything and expect them to feel the same way. We tell them we don't particularly care if they're *great* teachers yet, because if they work hard, we'll support them. They'll learn, and the children will learn.

Then we bombard them with questions. We ask questions that give us insight into the way that they'll respond to our distinct working environment. We want to know about their work ethic, their commitment to winning, their ability to work in trying conditions.

During the interview, most of my questions are designed not to elicit "correct" responses—but to *push*. I ask the candidates to teach me how to do a task—anything. I want to hear how they explain something that they care about. What I'm really listening for is passion. I want them to give me a cliff-hanger, leave me on the edge of my chair, wanting to know the rest of the story. In fact, sometimes I'll do just that: like my sons at bedtime, I'll ask them to tell me a story.

Most of all, I'm looking to be *entertained*. Seriously. If the teacher bores me in a conversation, I know that in a classroom setting, my kids are going to *crush* him.

The following are some of Capital Prep's actual interview questions:

1. Are you a good teacher? Prove it:
   a. Produce evidence that you can teach.
   b. Teach me how to do something.

2. What would be your reaction to 20 percent of your students failing an assignment?

3. Tell me why I should care about your subject.

4. Our school's theme is social justice—tell me how you will integrate it into your lessons.

5. We have mandatory after-school activities—tell me which ones you will lead and why they are important.

6. Explain how you create a lesson plan and a teaching unit.

7. We win here at Capital Prep—prove that you are a winner.

8. All of my kids are going to college—how are you going to ensure that that happens?

9. We are a year-round school—tell me your thoughts about a twelve-month school year.

10. What do you do in your free time?

Yes, the interview is confrontational, because we need to know how candidates handle stress. Teaching kids is stressful, and we don't need any punks. The last thing we are interested in is coming into teachers' classes to save them from our kids! We need to know that our teachers can handle themselves. Then we need them to know that we mean business. We can be their best friends once we see they're giving our kids everything they have. We also need them to understand from the gate that if they let us down, we let them go.

We are looking for attractive, smart, interesting people. Yes, I said *attractive*. Why? Because attractive, smart, and interesting people sell kids everything—from breakfast cereal to Xbox games. That may sound cynical, but it's the truth. Why should we expect anything different when trying to sell children education? Attractive reflects a presence more than an aesthetic. It's more than being "cute," it's about being compelling.

What am I looking for in prospective teachers' answers? Question by question by question:

1. I ask candidates to produce evidence they can teach because I want to hear specific examples of something they have done that proves kids learned because of them.

2. I ask candidates how they'd react if 20 percent of their students failed on an assignment because I want to hear that they care that *all* their students succeed. I don't want them to tell me that a 20 percent failure rate is acceptable. They have to own that type of failure and not put it on the kids. They have to tell me that they are going to be personally af-

fected and will spend the time before the next class obsessing over the significant failure. I ultimately want to know that I don't have to hold their hands and give them a big "You'll get 'em next time" speech.

3. I ask them why I should care about their subject because I want to know that they can "sell" a lesson, and themselves. A teacher has to stand in front of children of all ages and convince them that they need to listen for anywhere from forty-five to ninety minutes. The kids' instinct tells them to ask why. "Because I said so" is a weak answer. So I need to see that the teacher knows a really good reason why twenty-four kids who want to goof around after lunch break need to sit still—and pay attention—during chemistry.

4. I ask candidates how they would integrate our school's theme of social justice into their lessons because they need to show me that they believe in the school's theme. The best way they can do this is to bring up examples from their life.

5. I hire as many coaches as I can. A good coach can take huge concepts and break them down into discrete "blocks" that an unathletic kid can do with confidence. A good teacher does the same thing in the classroom. This is a chance for candidates to show me how they would coach, even if they've never done so. It's a tough process that I deeply respect and have seen work with kids from all walks of life.

6. I ask candidates to tell me how they create a lesson plan because I want to get a sense of how they think. There's no right answer.

7. My asking candidates to prove they are winners is self-explanatory. Losers lose. Winners win at all costs. We are playing for kids' lives. Losing is not an option.

8. Again, asking candidates how they will ensure that all Capital's kids go to college is about commitment to our purpose. It's also a way to see if a prospective teacher understands that everyone on staff has the responsibility to send kids to college.

9. I ask candidates to tell me what they think about Capital Prep's being a year-round school because I want to know that they share our beliefs. Being a good teacher is just the tip of the iceberg. We need our teachers to be committed to what we do. A candidate could be a good teacher but a bad fit for Capital Prep. The sooner we know this, the better.

10. I ask candidates what they do in their free time because their answer is crucial: people who love kids spend their free time with kids—coaching, teaching dance or gymnastics, tutoring, teaching Sunday school or Hebrew school. I just want to know that the candidate has the temperament to be a teacher.

It's no mystery why we have been successful here at Capital Prep. We've found great teachers who fit our system, who share our core beliefs that all of our children can go to college, and who are committed to our school theme of social justice. When they aren't great or don't fit, they're asked to leave. When they're great teachers and fit, we do everything imaginable to keep them on staff.

Public schools need to be open to the most talented educators. Talent and commitment must be the only determinants of who teaches our children. Kids have already had enough disadvantages heaped on them. Let's give them an opportunity to live a good life. They're not asking for a handout. They just want—and deserve—an honest chance at the best American education we can offer.

The first step in fulfilling the promise of a great American education is to put a great teacher in front of them.

We know what makes a good teacher. The challenge is convincing bad teachers that they are bad—then making their principals *do* something about it.

Anatomy of a Good Lesson

A GOOD LESSON is like a good song. It has a distinctive rhythm. It has a catchy hook. Its repetition can teach something that might take a lifetime to comprehend. In three minutes and a few seconds, skilled songwriters convey the emotions of falling in love, partying like it's 1999, or imagining all the people, living life in peace. . . .

If you're musically inclined, maybe you can appreciate a song by just reading the sheet music. But most of us require the interwoven elements of songwriter and performer. And it's much the same in the classroom: the written lesson and the teacher both need to be effective.

Writing a good lesson is a skill unto itself. Not every educator can pull it off. Constructing a lesson plan requires a clear understanding of the subject, the audience, the objective, and the competencies of the teacher as a teacher, learner, and performer. All of this must then be aligned with the state's or school's standards as well as the school's theme. The more in sync the alignments, the greater the probability that the lesson will be reinforced throughout the day, week, and year. Repetition improves the probability that the lesson will be internalized and learned by the students. A series of these lessons makes a solid unit. Units become a semester, so you can see that these lessons are the building blocks for an effective school curriculum.

Just because teachers can write a good lesson doesn't mean they can deliver. Many successful songwriters couldn't read music—some couldn't even carry a tune. In the 1960s, the legendary team of Lamont Dozier, Eddie Holland, and Brian Holland moved to Detroit and almost single-handedly authored the Motown sound. Sure, they did have minor careers as solo recording artists, but the team's songwriting is best known to us today through the records of groups like the Supremes, Martha and the Vandellas, and the Four Tops. Holland-Dozier-Holland had the formula down pat: they wrote simple lyrics over a constant repetition of the song's hook line—"Baby Love," "Stop! In the Name of Love," "You Can't Hurry Love," "It's the Same Old Song" . . .

For every hit-making team like Holland-Dozier-Holland, there are hundreds of talented songwriters who never made it past open-mike gigs at coffeehouses and never sold even one of their tunes. . . .

Similarly, I have seen teachers who can write the hell out of a lesson plan but simply don't connect with kids. They don't have the soul to *sell* the lesson. Throughout, the teacher struggles to keep the kids' attention. Reading the lesson plan beforehand, you'd think the teacher would kill when she got into class. The objective is clear; the assessments build toward a big finish. The activities are fun, and the teacher clearly knows her stuff. The problem is that not one kid is listening.

These days, shows like *American Idol* and *America's Got Talent* reel in tens of millions of viewers each week showcasing young singers—impassioned interpreters—part of a long tradition of performers who know how to *sell* a song. Do they write the music and lyrics that they sing? Nope. But who cares? It's entertaining.

Many schools have an established curriculum. The lesson plans are derived from a book of lessons that the school considers exemplary. And, fortunately, many teachers' ability to deliver a lesson is greater than their ability to write a solid lesson plan. That they're weak in the latter respect could be because they're brand-new teachers or simply veterans teaching sections other than those they typically teach. For example, I sometimes need an algebra teacher to take a section of geometry. Maybe he hasn't taught geometry in years but, if he's a good teacher and I can get him some solidly written lesson plans, the kids win. Good teacher meets good lesson plans equals compelling lessons.

Good lessons and songs ultimately inspire. The mind and heart react to the same stimuli—a motivated messenger. Aligning the hearts and minds of students should be the goal, and the means should be writing *and* performing good lessons.

Parents' Guide to Lesson Plans

A lesson plan is usually an indication of the quality of instruction. Unfortunately, very few teachers are actually required to turn one in, and you're not likely going to ever see your child's teachers' lesson plans. Nonetheless, you'll be able to discern if there is a lesson plan when you visit your child's class.

There are six crucial things to look for in a lesson plan, as illustrated in the following examples from a lesson on writing a thesis statement.

1. The lesson has a stated objective that is clear and measurable.

   Example: *Students will be able to write a thesis statement, as evidenced by their ability to complete a statement that predicts the direction of the essay.*

2. The lesson activities are designed to support fulfillment of the objective.

   Example: *Students read well-written thesis statements and the first few following paragraphs.*

3. The lesson activities appear to be appropriately timed.

   Example: *No activity seems to take too long. Each activity feels as if it ends just as all students have achieved an anticipated level of understanding.*

4. One activity transitions to the next with a logical flow.

   Example: *Students start by reading exemplars of thesis statements. Next, from their seats, they explain what they have read. They then turn to their neighbor and discuss what they have written. Finally, report back to the class.*

5. There are periodic assessments of the students' accomplishment of the objective.

   Example: *The teacher hands out an overview of elements that students use to evaluate their partner's thesis statement. When both students have scored at least an 80 per-*

cent, they move on to reporting out. When a student reports out, she is simply "reporting" verbally what she has learned. "Reporting out" is a form of assessment because the teacher gets to hear where each student is as he or she moves toward fulfilling the objective.

6. There is a clear, linear, and logical order to the class.

Example: *The lesson begins with an initiation that introduces or defines a thesis statement. Each subsequent progression is chunked into reasonable sections and culminates in the fulfillment of the objective.*

Thriller

AS CNN'S EDUCATION contributor, I regularly field questions from parents during our popular iReports feature. Probably the most common question I get from parents is how to get children more engaged in the learning process.

I have a simple answer. Learning—must—be *fun*.

But first let me say, your questions, as parents, aren't unique. From the 'burbs to the 'hood, we've lost an entire generation of American students to the scourge of failing public schools. Apathetic and outperformed, full of potential and hemorrhaging opportunities, our kids are spectators at a game in which they are dressed to play. American students should be winning. We spend a spectacular amount of money on education. Most communities commit as much as 80 percent of local property taxes to our public schools. Even in the 'hood, failure is costing us a fortune. Yet our kids can't compete with similar students internationally.

As evidenced by the constant stream of parents' questions to me on iReports, our kids have no *zeal* for learning. School is something to coast through until the freedom of summer. School is more social rite of passage than academic commitment. Or in kids' own words: straight-up *boring*. For years we've clung to a classics-based curriculum in which text and techniques from dead and dying generations are being forced upon a generation that buzzes. This generation of students isn't prepared to improve on the technology they can't seem to live without because they have not connected to the out-of-date methods we've used to teach them the basics.

Have you been to a school lately? Have you sat through the six hours and forty-five minutes of excruciating tedium we send our kids to every day? Have you seen our uninspired teachers pretend to engage our uninspired kids? It's painful to watch. When we ask our kids, "What'd you do in school today?" and they mumble "Nothin'," they're telling the truth. Our kids' funky attitude is supported by research confirming that in the average day, they do "nothing that inspires" or "nothing they can remember."

Not long ago, I interviewed a student in Manchester, New Hampshire, as part of a shoot for CNN's "Perry's Principles" that focused on dropout prevention programs that work. Chris missed ninety days of school during his first freshman year. By his *third* go-round as a freshman, he decided to drop out. I asked him why he skipped school. Chris is a bright kid. A reader. He has favorite books and some books that he can't stand, but books are in his life. He said that he didn't connect to school. Instead he just ditched class and wandered around outside the school in some nearby woods. Why? Because, as he said, he felt like he was being fed a plate of food he didn't like. So he didn't eat.

When I met Chris, he was a twenty-one-year-old high school "senior." He was in an alternative program call PASS—Program Alternative to Secondary School. Finally, he said, he had connected to the hands-on approach to learning. As I came in to talk to him, Chris was "building" a house, using computer-aided design (CAD) in a classroom that could have doubled for NASA's mission control center for all the cutting-edge technology on display. The PASS program took him from being disconnected from school to wanting to be a teacher! This insightful young man made it clear that when the curriculum is engaging, even the most disengaged students will choose to learn. Chris told me that he'd always liked to learn but had just never been offered a dish he could stomach.

That a kid with the advantages Chris has—suburban, White, and from a two-parent household—can't connect to our schools highlights the gaping holes in our broken public education system. Students need to be connected to their learning environment. The proper "fit" determines a child's level of success. When kids are connected to their school, they're likely to perform better. All children are not A students, of course, but all students can learn.

Disconnected kids hurt. It's a deep, often hidden pain. They feel like something is wrong with them. They feel utterly isolated from their teachers and their friends. Kids are cold and disrespectful to educators they feel are disrespectful toward them. When a teacher asks a student to read aloud even though he knows that the child struggles with reading, this is universally seen by students as a sign of disrespect. The level of pushback toward the teacher is directly related to the type of personality the student has. Kids who are quiet and reserved will retreat, maybe even to the point of not speaking. More belligerent kids will curse out the teacher.

Chris is more typical than not. He felt like his teachers didn't care. Therefore, he reasoned, why the hell should he care? In all fairness, his teacher may have been phenomenal, but Chris is the kind of kid who likes to learn with his hands. Few traditional schools these days offer tactile learning. Chris may simply represent an example of the wrong kid at the wrong school.

A disconnect between student and school can have a profoundly negative effect. Children's confidence can suffer and their desire to get an education can be stamped out. Kids quit school in many ways. Some leave abruptly, as if making a bold statement to the world, while others are more likely to just drift by, semester after semester. These kids are the ones who have so much potential but, for some reason, won't bear down. These kids confound us because we don't look at the obvious: the school itself is wrong for them. Our kids say it so often that we think they're just being teenagers who hate everything. That's part of it, of course, but most kids are telling the truth. The just don't have the sophistication to express it. So we think they're just teenage whiners or lazy slackers, when, in fact, they're expressive, thoughtful young people who aren't built to travel with the herd.

I've seen the right students and the wrong students come to Capital Prep. We're heavy on discipline. Some kids crave this. They love our in-your-face, take-no-prisoners approach, while others hate it. The latter feel like they are in prison, being robbed of their freedom, while the former feel alive and somehow free for the first time in their school lives. Oddly enough, both types of student are right.

Every day that a student spends in the wrong school is excruciating for us all. Waking such students up is a chore. Getting them to do their homework is a nightmare. Getting them to do well is a seemingly infinite push and pull. Our traditional schools cannot be all things to all students. When students are in the right school studying what inspires them, it's an awesome thing to behold. They wake up without a parent having to pour a cold glass of water on them. (Yes, one of my parents had to literally do this each morning because we were the wrong school for her system-bucking daughter.) You won't have to threaten or bribe them to do homework. When the right kids are in the right school, we all feel proud.

Veteran teachers are often heard saying that kids are different than they were a generation ago. They're right. Then why in the hell are we trying to teach today's students the same way that we taught their grandparents? Same books, same strategies, different results. Today's kids aren't interested and aren't producing. Their basic skills don't match those of the generations before and it's not their fault.

Today's educators blame standardized tests for the flattening of the curriculum. Standardized tests didn't force schools to give up on the beauty of learning for learning's sake or cause them to fall back on unimaginative, uncreative lesson plans. That's like blaming the bathroom scale for your cocktail dress being too tight. It's not the *tests*. It's the curriculum, stupid. . . .

We're losing the fire that our children bring into school because we've made no fundamental changes to the way in which schools have operated for generations. According to a McKinsey report, the longer American children are in school, the worse they perform compared to their international peers. Still, parents send the children who are their legacy into the rain, sleet, heat, and snow to catch the bus to a bright future. Parents' hopes disappear in the yawning achievement gap.

It's like we've stuffed this generation into our great-great-grandmothers' corsets and are trying to pass it off as "vintage" chic. The kids know that it's just old and stinks. They don't do well in our schools because our schools don't meet their academic and our economy's needs.

But make no mistake: real educational innovation is happening in this country. The most exciting educators, like Harlem's Geoffrey Canada, live and work in some of the country's most economically deprived neighborhoods. Suburban parents need to encourage suburban educators to make a pilgrimage to their nearest successful urban school to figure out how in the hell we've been able to take children from historically disadvantaged populations and get them into the same colleges as their advantaged students. When we calculate the distance traveled, the kids in the 'hood's successful schools have grown more and gone further than those in the suburbs—because their schools are better designed and are operating with more effective leaders and educators.

Most public schools are using the same old didactic approach to teaching and learning that we've always used. The teacher stands at the front of the class. He talks and writes on the board; the students listen and write. That's it. This style of teaching and learning is lost on most of the over 65 million kids who are in a public school today. It makes no damned sense to think that one type of anything can serve so many diverse people. Kids can't even agree about their favorite music, jeans, or sneakers, but they can agree that the way we're teaching them isn't working to engage them.

In the suburbs, educators can't complain about resource gaps. Sure, there are a few differences between ultrawealthy suburbs and middle-class suburbs, but for the most part, all have access to the best technology. Suburban kids have plenty of books. Suburban schools tend not to be crumbling and decrepit. The children come from relatively supportive homes. The parents do homework with their kids. They read along with them. They attend all the games. These are what teachers call the "ideal conditions" for education. So why are Korea, Finland, and two dozen other nations making even our middle-class *suburban* children look like they live in the 'hood?

KIDS DON'T NEED bells and whistles to learn. A piano is a piano. Learning to play requires the same techniques that have been used since the instrument was invented. Where many children lose interest is in the selection of music. Teachers teach what they know how to play and value the way they learned how to play it. Inherently, there is a generational gap between teacher and student. The teacher grew up on Bach, the Beatles, and the Bee Gees, and these students are bumpin' Lil Wayne, Jay-Z, and Alicia Keys.

Our lessons tell kids whether we teach to make a living or because it's something we truly love. When kids feel like a teacher has put time into creating an assignment, they're more likely to put care into doing it right. Kids are really no different from educators. We reward effort, even when the product is lacking.

A while back, my wife and I were on a layover at the airport in Charlotte, North Carolina. When she went to the ladies' room, there was a bathroom attendant singing "You are my sunshine . . ." As women came in and out of stalls, wrestled with infants, and generally tried to avoid eye contact in this most familiar and awkward of places, they were greeted by the bathroom attendant. Bright and bubbly, she pointed out open stalls and encouraged all who came to do their business to remember that "It's not where you work—it's *how* you work."

Kids are kids. That only makes them young—not stupid. They intuitively know that they need inspiration and we know that they deserve it. When educators set out to design schools that inspire, all the individual pieces become inspirational.

The fundamentals of arithmetic haven't changed since the beginning of recorded history; four plus four will always equal eight. The reason that many students don't connect with the subjects they're supposed to be learning is because the lessons lack relevance and rigor. We can more effectively teach children to count when we're teaching them to count something that is relevant to them.

Once a piano teacher accepts that the last great song hasn't been written, he can accept that there might be contemporary music that matters as much as the classics, just-released pop music from which students can learn the techniques necessary to be a solid musician. Good teachers know how to "flip the script." As I'll explain later, in the chapter "New Schools, Old Books," they can even use the catchy tunes from *The Lion King* to explore the tragedy of *Hamlet*.

Which brings me to my own sons and their struggle with the baby grand piano in our living room. When I was growing up, all the high-achieving (mostly White) kids I knew took mandatory piano lessons. To me, it seemed that learning Beethoven and Haydn went hand in hand with future success in higher education. So I signed my boys up.

For a couple of years now, Walker, five, and Mason, eight, have taken piano lessons. Every Sunday morning from ten to eleven, "Mr. Ronald" Hawkins, with my help, tried to get my sons to focus on learning to play "Hot Cross Buns" and "Mary Had a Little Lamb." Politely impatient, Mr. Ronald plodded through the lessons. I was embarrassed and angry at my sons and my wife for their lack of focus, clenching my teeth at every distant gaze my sons displayed or ridiculous question they asked. Fueled by my humiliation, I spent weeknights drilling my sons well into the night.

Amid the coverage of the death of Michael Jackson, my boys discovered him and soon filled our home and their time with the late singer's music. Then one Saturday morning, I heard my oldest teaching himself to play Michael Jackson's "Thriller." I sat in the other room amazed. I thought he hated the piano and was on the verge of hating me. But for twenty minutes he plunked the keys, plodding through his frustration and his little brother's persistent reminders that "That's not how it goes . . ."

I asked Mr. Ronald to teach Mason to play Michael Jackson. We had no sheet music of the Jackson Five or Jackson's solo catalogue, so Mason went online and listened to the songs, picking up what he could. When Mr. Ronald came over with a Michael Jackson songbook, it was like Christmas in July! While Walker volunteered to go first, Mason disappeared into his room with his new book, shopping for the song he was going to play first. When Mason practiced, Walker danced until I sent him out of the room. Walker later returned with two plastic shovels to declare that he would practice "Beat It" on the *drums*.

No, we don't have drums, but who cares? He was into it.

Walker still struggled through his lesson, which covered such things as bars, meter, and half and quarter notes. And Mason's left hand is still not as dexterous as it needs to be, but they both want to learn to play the piano today because they *connect* to the content. We laughed and the kids had fun! Yes, learning can be fun.

For that one hour, no one had to be told to focus. In fact, Mr. Ronald cautioned Mason that he was *too* serious. Too serious? My eight-year-old son, who can't sit still for eight seconds, was suddenly too serious? Before he bought the books, Mr. Ronald told me that the songs were above my sons' ability to play. He was right, but the thing is, the boys don't know that. Walker will learn his bars and quarter notes, Mason's left hand will improve, and I won't become Joe Jackson.

WHEN WE CAN step from behind our national insecurity, we will finally be able to operate the schools our children deserve and our nation needs. Our failure to live up to the highest standards of international achievement has cost us immensely. Remember that 2009 McKinsey report I cited earlier, with that stunning $1.3 trillion to $2.3 trillion that would have been added to our GDP if we could somehow have closed the education gap with nations like Finland and Korea?

Okay, if stats like that don't move you, then go to your doctor, or call computer tech support. Look for American-born pharmacy students, accountants, engineers, or any other highly skilled workers in emerging science, technology, or math-based fields. Our schools are designed to produce students who can be slotted into a manufacturing-based, industrialized economy, and they do. When the world needed bombers produced during and after World War II, America had things on lock. Now that we need people who can teach and use the sciences, we're at a loss.

Yet we adults can relate to and inspire kids. We're the ones who make the movies, video games, music, and toys that our children beg us to buy. Schools and school systems need to look beyond convention to learn how to connect with our kids.

On CNN, I've had the opportunity to interview two of the best-selling rappers and producers of all time. Between them, Sean "Diddy" Combs and Pharrell Williams have sold over 200 million records. What I wanted to know was pretty simple: how do they do it? I wanted each to explain to me how they connect with kids. There is much that we, parents and educators, can learn from entertainers. These folks keep our kids twisted around their blinged-out fingers.

Diddy and Pharrell spoke of how they begin with the goal of connecting to their audience. Interesting—this is the first question that we have our students answer when we are teaching them to write. We ask them to identify their audience, yet as educators, we are too often our own audience and so it's no wonder that our kids could care less. They're only mirroring our feelings toward them.

History didn't end when the history teacher graduated from college. So why not start with today and work your way back? For students interested in sports, teach math with the batting averages and shooting percentages in the sports section. Teach others using the stock market. Still others by having them remodel their room. One of the most popular geometry projects at Capital Prep is called "Extreme Room Makeover." In this multiple-week assignment, students have to build a mockup of their room. Some students go all out, even building three-dimensional models—showing a remarkable level of detail, even the posters, magazines, and books in the bedroom.

I can tell when a teacher has really hit the mark because the whole school is abuzz with the assignment. We had a biology assignment on DNA. Our first-year biology teacher, Mrs. Bray, knocked this one out of the park. Kids who visibly hated science, and sometimes school, were excited by the idea of "making" DNA. They used everything you can imagine: licorice and gumdrops, pipe cleaners, paper clips, wood, papier-mâché, cereal boxes. You name it—the building was filled with DNA!

As I mentioned, Capital Prep's theme is social justice. One of our math teachers was teaching probability. To teach racial profiling, he used jelly beans. Yes, jelly beans. This assignment required that students correctly and proportionately represent a community's racial makeup with a container of jelly beans. Once this was done, students shook up the container and simply reached in their hand to see how likely they were to pull out a Black or Latino jelly bean.

What was coolest about this assignment was that it was born out of a conversation between a history teacher and a math teacher. "Conversation" may be cleaning it up a little. It was a pretty heated exchange. The former history teacher is a Black woman, in her late sixties and from the South. The math teacher is a White male from a very affluent northern suburb. Ms. Ford was informing Mr. Kapralos of the issue of racial profiling. Having never experienced it personally, he struggled to accept that it was a real problem today. He went home that night, haunted by the realization that he might have a blind spot to a very serious social issue, a problem that—as a teacher in an 86 percent minority school—he needed to develop sensitivity toward.

Rather than grapple with it emotionally, he approached it through the lens of a field he knew intimately—mathematics. After reading some articles for background, he asked his almost all Black and Latino students, what's the probability of some 80 percent of the traffic offenses in a particular town being committed by an African American when the community's Black population is less than 12 percent?

At Capital Prep, we are moving toward electronic portfolios for all students. Students are encouraged to select work to be included in their "e-portfolio" that they feel best represents their growth and ability. Artifacts in the e-portfolio are assignments that matter most to the student. It's really not that important *what* the assignment is, but rather that the student can explain why the assignments are relevant. Typically, students pick work they're proud of (and that earned them a high grade) or that enables them to show tangible growth in a subject. What having students pick the work accomplishes is twofold. First, it allows the students to play an active role in tracking their learning. Second, it helps us identify teachers who create the greatest number of "meaningful" assignments.

When kids include an assignment in their e-portfolio, it helps us know what they *like* to do. Ironically, none of the assignments or teachers that I've just highlighted made our kids' top five. Our social worker, Mrs. Perry (no relation), who's been in the system for over twenty years, and Mr. Ali, a thirty-year social studies teacher, generated the most artifacts. What *I* think is cool and what the *kids* think is meaningful are vastly different. Neither Mrs. Perry nor Mr. Ali used technology in their assignments, yet the kids ate their assignments up! I was shocked. The two most senior staff, two teachers seemingly least likely to use technology and most removed generationally from our youngest students, created, as per the student data, the most artifacts, the most meaningful assignments last year.

What all these assignments have in common are faculty who pushed themselves to go beyond what they've done in the past to inspire themselves and the students. Also, the assignments the kids liked most were the most relevant.

We have an openly gay teacher, Ms. Davern, who taught a lesson on the Holocaust from a homosexual perspective. Remarkably, I got no calls at my office. We went to great pains to make sure that the Holocaust assignment was signed off on by parents, and I spoke with Ms. Davern at least three times before and after she delivered the lesson.

By contrast, Mr. Ali's assignment seemed pretty straightforward. In the midst of the 2008 presidential campaign, he asked the kids to go home and ask their parents their opinion of the campaigns and candidates. That interview was signed and turned in. Yet this was the most controversial assignment that we've had since the school opened, which is ironic because Mr. Ali is the least controversial human you'll ever meet.

When Mr. Ali asked the parents to do homework with the kids—*whew,* I got five parents calling from that one class. The superintendent's office wanted to talk to me about the assignment being "too political."

Schools have to be willing to take risks, because that's what kids want. They want to feel like this assignment matters to the teacher as much as it does to them. Kids can be inspired to learn—to go for something beyond getting a good grade. They can want to create a thought-provoking piece. Technology is an excellent tool to deliver a well-thought-out assignment. Yet nothing—and I mean absolutely nothing—takes the place of an inspired and prepared teacher.

And nothing will stop a student from becoming engaged—falling in love—with the learning process if the teacher can turn the assignment into a "Thriller."

The Principal

YOU NEED TO MEET your kids' principal. More than anyone else, this person could make or break your kid's academic experience. But it's not enough to meet him—I want to teach you how to identify a good principal. I want you to be able to determine if your child's principal has the capacity and sensibilities needed to lead the type of school you want your child to attend.*

First, you'll need some context for the role of the principal. Principals must accept full responsibility for the state of education. What happens in schools can—must—be influenced by a solid school leader. Sure, there are some schools that just seem to run themselves. It wouldn't matter if they hired a chimpanzee to be principal; the school would maintain its performance. Why? Certain positive traditions and habits have been ingrained, and the institution is running on autopilot. Yet, interestingly, even these high-functioning schools improve based on who's sitting in the principal's office.

Schools with the most breathtaking results have been inspired by an authentic leadership team. These schools are run by

---

*I recognize that many people in the United States currently don't have much choice in terms of available public schools. I'm advocating for school choice wherever choice is possible. Many rural children today have no real school choice. However, most American students living in cities and towns could have choice through vouchers. Until education vouchers become an accepted matter of public policy, what I'm describing in this chapter is an *ideal* that parents should fight for.

visionary leaders, adrenaline junkies who have ambitions beyond maximizing test scores; they want to change education. A great principal cannot beat a great team; a great principal builds one. She knows her strengths and embraces her weaknesses by identifying people who complement her.

The path to public education's meltdown has been blazed by average school leaders. Not horrible or ill-willed—just average administrators who are in way over their heads. These are the folks who have accepted and perpetuated the lie that *the union has made it impossible* to fire bad teachers. They are afraid of parents, negotiate punishments with students, and wait to be told what to think by the central office. Nice guys, for sure, but *bad* principals. Lackeys have filled the ranks of school administration. The last ones standing, they're decent dudes who paid their dues. They're good managers, homegrown homeboys—but they all sit in jobs that should only be occupied by the most energetic, determined people in the workforce. There's no job that requires a person to be more adroit in so many competencies than a school principal.

Principals must set the course for a school. Listen, I know as well as anybody how meddlesome the suits in the central office can be. It's plain ridiculous. Let's start with the "dynamic" nature of the superintendent's job. Between 2005, when we opened Capital Prep, and 2011, we've had four different superintendents. And during that same six-year period, I've had at least six supervisors. I say "at least" because, I have to confess, there were a few people I was *supposed* to be answering to whom I might have forgotten. Hell, I've had more immediate and obvious challenges. I have to run a school, chart a course, hire and evaluate talent, set budgets, deal with parents, and discipline kids as eleven different people supervise me for terms as short as six months.

I've gotten those silly-ass calls from some assistant superintendent looking to make his mark, questioning why we had to suspend a child. Then I had to spend one full day, literally, formally replying to his e-mails and calls. I take a child out of school for one day and the assistant superintendent effectively takes me out of action for one day. This, while the crisis around the district is real. This, while over 60 percent of the city's students are reading at least one grade below grade level. In the same year that 100 percent of our Capital Prep children achieved proficiency on the state's standardized writing tests, I've had to spend weeks writing reports that are never read by anyone.

I know what it's like to get a call from someone at the central office assigning me some busywork, some technocratic bull that has nothing at all to do with improving school performance. A bunch of folks with fancy titles downtown, some coordinator, director, assistant to the assistant of the universe, will send me ten e-mails requiring me to go online and complete a survey on whether or not the central office has helped us. No joke—or actually a *gigantic* joke—this is nothing more than the customer service survey you get after shopping online. Except there you have the option of clicking "No, thanks, I decline."

Nobody has to tell me that most of what the central office does is entirely self-serving. They've devised ways of wasting hundreds of hours on protecting the people who work in the central office, often in some made-up position with a fancy title, just so they can retain that position. Look, in most troubled school districts, Jesus himself could be appointed superintendent, with Moses and Muhammad as his assistant superintendents, and the system would still suck. The kids still wouldn't read or use a computer at grade level. The kids still wouldn't have the ingrained behaviors necessary to succeed in education. I've walked the walk for years now. I've worked in one of the nation's worst school districts. They are broken. As long as the structure is in place, the house will be too dangerous to occupy.

Failing districts are the seed from which the root of the oft-cited achievement gap has grown. Their existence promises a perpetuation of past pain and political pandering. These districts exist to feed the egos of adults while squashing the hopes of children. They are fatally flawed. Folks both deeply committed and simply passing through, capable and incompetent, have run school districts; good principals have run their schools; smart people have spent their careers teaching in them; and still they have produced no significant success.

Heavily centralized districts have been sued, and lost, then been taken over by the state, only to emerge phoenix-like from the ashes. The schools have been bused and desegregated, chartered, magnetized, and reorganized. Still, they have shown little more than marginal growth—3 percent here, 5 percent there—nothing close to the fundamental change needed to provide America's children the boost they need to catch up to the members of their international cohort.

Average principals simply accept what they're given. Superstar principals go get it. They don't accept the low-lying fruit of the status quo. They're unencumbered by supposed barriers. Race, class, parents' education, school location, unions, and bureaucracy are mere jungle vines through which they machete a path to academic success. Great principals are intolerant of excuses and focused on results.

The nation's best principals don't need a functional school district. They can build a breathtaking oasis in an educational desert.

So what can you do as a parent? You have to recognize those schools run by *leaders* versus ones run by *administrators*. What's the difference? An administrator maintains while a leader disrupts. The academic status quo is the death of progress. We're educating a generation for an economy that's two generations in the past. School leaders want to improve the school's performance and change the face of education. They embrace results-driving assessments, hire and fire based on a set of values in which the child—not the teacher's tenure—is central.

There are standout principals bubbling up all over the nation, ones who are making educational excellence seem easy to achieve, but these hard-charging educators are still rare. I've met talented principals in both the 'hood and the 'burbs, but too often the principals in the wealthiest suburbs are too caught up trying not to piss anyone off. They don't want anyone to blame them for blowing their school's reputation, so they stand down from confrontations. They let the system of rambunctious parents and politician superintendents tell them when and what to think.

It is too easy to think of suburban academic success or failure in comparison to urban districts' results. We have to look at our education as assessed by the end-product users. The suburban myth of success gives folks a sense of self-confidence that is, ultimately, hollow. Saying you beat the test scores of a poor minority school system in some statewide evaluation is like bragging that you marshaled your troops to overrun the Salvation Army.

Principals are, in a sense, the gatekeepers of America's elementary and secondary educational experience. Principals can be either the most important or the least important people in the building. Too often, we muddle through our day's work or spend hours jumping from crisis to crisis. In the end, we become little more than guardrails on education's highway.

On the other hand, when we set a clear vision and hold the entire team to it, we can be those big green destination signs on the drive toward success. We are the reason that people want to work at our schools. We act as "dad" when children have none; we are "mom" sometimes even when they have one. When we, as principals, are focused and capable, we are the most important people in the school.

You want your children's school run by a principal who can align parents and students, inspire adults, and beat back the ever-changing whims of the board of education. A capable principal is the only professional positioned to save thousands of lives per day.

Parents, take charge. Today. Get to know the principal at your kids' school.

PART FOUR

Parenting

Dazed and Confused

LET'S GET IT straight: schools are failing because of the people who work in them, not because of parents like you. The truth is that *one* factor—teacher effectiveness—has the greatest impact on student performance.

As parents, you need to understand what you can and cannot impact. And then you must take responsibility for that which is yours. Relinquish your parental guilt. Let it *go*. Once you know the truth about our schools, you will more effectively support your kids' education.

In a September 2010 *Time* magazine poll, 52 percent of the respondents believed that "more involved parents" would improve students' performance. Only 24 percent believed that "more effective" teachers would improve students' performance. Also, a paltry 6 percent thought that the answer would be found in a longer school day.

Nothing improves student performance as much as quality of instruction. The lion's share of the blame must rest squarely upon the shoulders of educators like me. No, parents are neither the cause nor the solution for the problems in our schools. Teachers and the amount of time that students spend on instruction are what improve student performance. In fact, the entire *parents need to be more involved* argument is a blunt instrument most often used to bludgeon families into accepting blame for educators' failings.

Even if parent participation did improve student performance, few schools would ever reap the benefits. Now, listen, the principal in me knows that some parents are never coming to anything. In fact, I bet if we scheduled the school play in their own living room, they'd still have an excuse for missing it. Most parents aren't like this, though. Most feel so compelled to be a good parent that they become a bad employee.

Every parent who has to work is working. Schools often make frantic parents feel worse by making parental participation so difficult. Yeah, I'm a principal, but I'm a father, too. I hate when my sons' school schedules performances during the school day because when I can't go, which too often happens, my kids and I are hurt by my absence. It's just damn cruel.

I'm so sick of hearing educators claim that we don't know how to get parents to participate in their children's education. If we really want to maximize parental participation, then we should start by scheduling activities when most parents can come.

Open houses are one example of public schools' bait and switch. When we schedule the open house, we know that there won't be enough time or room for all the students' parents. Still, we make it seem like the end of the world if you don't come.

We herd you into a room full of equally anxious families as younger siblings wrestle over chocolate chip cookies. Then we speed though a goofy fifteen-minute presentation that's billed as an overview of our classes. As questions swirl in your head, you're boxed out by the obnoxious know-it-all formerly home-schooling couple who ask the most obscure questions in an effort to prove how smart they are.

Many public schools have *no* intention of accommodating all the parents at their open houses. Think about it: In an elementary school classroom there are typically twenty students who sit in twenty tiny elementary school chairs. A class with twenty kids has at least forty biological parents. And that's not including the step-parents, grandparents, guardians, brothers, or sisters who might be coming to the open house. How in the hell are over forty adults and younger siblings gonna sit in an elementary school classroom?

In private college preparatory schools, parents are needed— for financial support—and they're treated like it. Calendars are crowded with grandparents' days, mothers' days, fathers' days, reading days, family weekends, and dinners with the headmaster or with the deans on campus. Each activity is designed to foster meaningful relationships between educators and adults in the home. These opportunities to be on campus are in addition to all the sports and theater productions that teachers at private schools are required to attend.

It's often said that parents in private schools are more involved than those in public schools. I can't confirm this. I don't think anybody can. What is clear is that the more money parents make, the more likely they're going to be invited to campus. This formula is even the case in the public schools. Man, let us find out that a kid's family has dough and we're calling them to come speak, participate on a board, or whatever we can get them to do. By the same token, ain't *nobody* calling a broke parent of any color for anything unless it's absolutely necessary.

We're a public school, so I can't make teachers do *jack* after school hours. Public school teachers' contracts limit the number of open houses per year to two, lasting no more than two hours each. Any other school activity is optional for teachers. If I want my teachers running after-school activities, including additional parent activities, I've got to pay them overtime. So the most convenient times for parents are often the most expensive times for schools.

I don't want to hear that educators don't understand parents. Most of us *are* parents. We have to deal with the challenges of working and participating in our kids' school. This should make us empathetic to the complications of working and parenting—in that order. We know that doing something as simple as varying the schedule could increase our own participation in our kids' school, so why wouldn't it work to increase participation for our students' parents?

Parents, especially the good ones, feel inadequate. Educators know that you're in a constant state of confusion, wondering if you've gone too far—or not far enough. We hear your questions, exposing your insecurities about your parenting. You want to know if taking your son off the football team might improve his grades. You ask us if we think your seven-year-old really needs a cell phone. You want to know how much time is too much on the Internet. And whether there's really that much scholarship money out there that a kid can actually get a scholarship for being left-handed. And we've had to tell you, yes, if you're a left-handed *pitcher* and can throw a 98 mph fastball . . .

Parents, you have so many questions that you often feel stupid. You feel as though you should know—or worse, that everybody else knows. But educating a child is complicated even for educators who are parents. You'd be shocked how clueless educators can be when they're returning as parents.

Education is the biggest blind spot for parents. It doesn't matter how much·schooling you've had, you're not trained to teach algebra, physics, or Shakespeare.

With little more than a parent's instinct and a community's rumors, you move to the best school district you can afford. Even when your plan is to send your child to private school, you still want to live in a community where the schools are believed to be better. You know that everything from the value of your home to the quality of your kids' play dates is impacted by a community's schools. You hope that once you've chosen the community with the best schools, your family will cruise into a bright future.

The problem is that we are a nation of the wrong schools.

Educators see parents struggling every day. We should offer you a shoulder, lend an ear, tell you a story about another parent we heard from/talked to last week who had the same issue. Instead, we let you feel like your child and your family are the only ones dealing with the problem.

Schools need to do a better job of responding to parents. There's too much technology and too many known strategies for parents' questions to go unanswered.

Some things parents should expect from their kids' school:

- You should expect a call back from your child's teacher within twenty-four hours. They're busy, but not *that* busy.

- You should have a syllabus to support your disorganized teenage son.

- If a school is going to identify your child as having special needs, then you have a legal right to a PPT—a planning and placement team. This is a meeting in which teachers, administrators, and counselors come together to help parents identify strategies to address a child's perceived issues. The PPT should take as long as it takes for you to get your questions answered about the life-altering decisions that are about to be made.

- Patience. We could make you feel so much better by being patient with all your questions and telling you the truth.

Too many of you simply stop asking. The weeds that suffocate public schools grow in the absence of parents' questions. This is the space in which lies become truths and myths become traditions.

There is a difference between asking an honest question and the belligerence that many educators experience from parents. It's our challenge to ensure that we do our level best to not take the anger and hurt personally and to really *hear* why the parent is pissing vinegar. Sometimes listening is difficult, but that doesn't make it any less important.

Questions make us all grow. We derive some of our greatest growth from a sincere question. When you ask why a particular policy is in place, you deserve an answer, not an excuse. Tradition is irrelevant, since circumstances are always changing.

You're due answers on homework policies and staff evaluation processes just as you have a right to sit on a committee that hires staff. No, you cannot expect a specific answer about discipline handed out to another parent's child, but you can ask for the rationale for the discipline that was handed down to yours.

You have rights. You never have to go to a meeting with the school by yourself. Bring an advocate who can help you understand and support you. PPTs shouldn't be intimidating. We're supposed to be there to correct issues, not create lingering phobias. While I will discuss many of these issues throughout the book, the takeaway is that the problem isn't you. There is an effort to keep parents in the dark in many schools.

Many schools don't really know how to make the parent a useful partner. It's just not in their structural DNA. The conversation about school reform needs to begin by relieving parents of the burden of the school district. We've made you accept guilt because it absolves us of our accountability. When you don't understand how a child is supposed to complete his Spanish homework, it's not your fault. You don't teach Spanish, so how would you know the appropriate use of the imperfect tense?

Educators can decipher the code. We can explain the college application process and make you feel like a smart and valued partner. We can assist you if you want to do extra things to help your kids with reading. We don't have to wait until a child is failing to notify you that there's an issue. On the day that we're grading quizzes and we put an "F" on the page, you should be notified. Then we need to explain what we were looking for when we handed out the assignment.

Technology has opened up the door to a virtually seamless and transparent school-home relationship. A number of data systems exist that give parents real-time access to grades, behavior, and, in some cases, actual video of the learning process. I say, rip the doors off the schools so that we can clarify the process. You should be able to watch your child learn. He is your child. We don't have anything to hide. Log in. The world watched as the BP blowout poured millions of gallons of crude into the Gulf. If we can run cameras miles below the ocean's surface, then why can't we mount them in the classrooms? This is *public* education.

I meet bright, well-educated parents struggling to understand the process of education. When parents are lost, they react. They withdraw or become belligerent. Neither response helps the kids or the parent. When we show a good-faith effort to open up the educational process to parents, more parents will participate. Like their children, when parents feel unwanted, they're not productive.

It doesn't take much to make parents feel welcome. A vase of flowers on the receptionist's desk, a comfortable place to sit while they wait, and polite people answering the phone—all go a long way to improving parent-school relations. While open houses have a place, they shouldn't supplant meaningful creative strategies for parental engagement. Plan something just for the parents. For example, a parents' prom that plays songs from their respective eras, or bingo or a cookout. If these don't work, we've got to keep trying.

I've spent too many nights with the same five committed, involved parents at Capital Prep. The same five parents who come to *everything*. Too many nights I've been frustrated, knowing that my kids and wife are at home while I sit at the school with a bowl of punch that's as still as Jell-O. But this is the life I've chosen. I've got to work with all parents. I've got your kids. The rest is academic.

....

Five Things Parents Can Control

1. *Early reading.* All parents can read to kids, even if it's in another language. The very act of a parent and child reading together is powerful on many levels. Statistics show that kids who read with parents have advantages in life—higher earnings, more stable marriages, even better overall health.

2. *Early numeracy.* Parents have to expose children to math earlier. Counting and simple addition are just the beginning. Parents can instill academic courage in children by exploding the perception that being good at math is God given and that being bad at it is okay.

3. *Setting high expectations.* Parents can and must chart the course of their child's life. No matter what your kids want to be when they grow up, it is up to you to start the conversation that they be *something.*

4. *Curiosity.* Through free trips to the library and local museums, even virtual tours on the Internet, parents can instill in their children an intellectual curiosity that will serve the kids well into adulthood.

5. *Discipline.* Junk in, junk out. When you send us a kid who can't sit still and offer nothing more than excuses as to why this is so, you are setting everybody up for failure. Parents must make sure that their kids can deal with the reasonable expectations of a classroom.

....

Five Things for Which Parents Are Blamed but Can't Control

1. *Test scores.* Low test scores are the result of poor instruction. Neither parents nor tests are to blame. Low test scores are the school's fault. We know what is on the tests, and when kids are not prepared, it is because we did not prepare them.

2. *School violence.* When the adults run the building, the children feel safe. When kids feel safe, they don't act violently. Schools that fail to control children have children who are out of control.

3. *Dropout rates.* Schools that suck have high numbers of kids who drop out. Schools that make kids feel unloved and disconnected have kids who become withdrawn and ultimately withdraw. Schools, especially those in the 'hood, that provide a rich wraparound academic and social experience have high retention, graduation, and achievement rates. In the best of these schools, kids refer to the school as a family.

4. *Truancy.* A parent can make kids get out of bed, drop them off at the school, and watch them go in the door. They cannot make them stay. That's on us. When schools have created an intellectually rich, socially safe environment where kids can be happy, kids come to school. Great schools don't have truancy problems, because kids want to be there.

5. *The condition of the schools.* The state of public education is the result of the failings of educators. Public school teachers

and administrators have gotten away with murder for over a generation. We've had free rein over America's future and, like the financial markets, we have blundered on an epic scale. The condition of public schools is the result of public school educators' failings.

....

Adults vs. Parents

THERE IS A DIFFERENCE between adults and parents. Too often, being an adult means doing whatever you can get away with to make yourself happy. Being a parent means putting your kids' needs above your compulsions of adulthood. It's an ongoing conflict—taking care of your kids without losing the inner child that's in every well-adjusted adult.

I need more *parents* in my life. I've got way too many adults. These folks care too much about their weekend plans to be at their son's football game. I got into this business of working with kids because I can't stand working with adults.

When principals have access to *parents*, it's much easier to create a school culture in which both child and parent think of school as a fun place. When parents are in the building, they're working to create a warm, comfortable place where their children can build lasting relationships while developing skills essential to their future endeavors. The years from childhood through adolescence are the most dynamic, and arguably difficult, in one's life.

Adults want to be their kids' friends. Parents monitor their kids' friends.

Kids don't want their parents to be their friends. You don't need to tell your children that they can talk to you about anything, because they're not *supposed* to be able to talk to you about anything. You're not a friend friend! Do you really want your daughter asking you about the best way to perform oral sex?

Your children need you to establish a comfortable distance from them within which they'll retain a sense of safety. The more you act like your kids, the less they'll trust your judgment.

No son wants to have to coordinate his weekends to avoid ending up at the same house party as his divorced dad. Teenage girls don't want their mom borrowing their clothes. They don't want you to know the words to their generation's sound track. Kids don't want you in their space—that's why MySpace was a hit when it launched. When parents invaded and made MySpace corny, the kids disappeared into Facebook, Twitter, Tumblr, and farther and farther into the backwoods of the Internet, always two steps ahead of these grown-ups, tapping away on their keyboards in a sad desire to hook up with former high school sweethearts.

You've had your chance to live that lifestyle—remember Fort Lauderdale, spring break 1994? Now fall back, *Homes*. Hate to break it to you, but the New Kids on the Block and the Backstreet Boys are gray-haired and balding. It's time for you to start chaperoning trips to the concert, but not actually jumping into the mosh pit. The rest of your days as a fan are supposed to be spent at an '80s hair-band revival or on a summer lawn at a free jazz concert.

At work you hear horror stories from your colleagues about their kids' bad decisions. This one has failing grades; that one is dating a guy who's already in college; that one had some weed in his jeans pocket. . . . You're not sure if you should run home and mount a preemptive strike or wait until your kid comes to you.

And what if he does? Are you even equipped to deal with what he's got to say?

Being an adult means not even concerning yourself with these things. Being a *parent* means you can't stop being concerned. A good mom, for example, can't help but wonder if she has a close enough relationship with her daughter for her to feel comfortable coming to Mom when her boyfriend wants to have sex. Such a mom wonders quite a bit if she should bring up the conversation with her daughter about sexuality or just wait. Is the daughter being bullied, and if she is, will she feel comfortable telling her mom?

You have every right to be concerned with struggles such as this. I see too much to tell you there's nothing to worry about. Too many kids both lose their virginity and become parents at the same time. Too many parents find out too late that their son wasn't just having a bad semester, he was depressed. How did they know? He told them in his suicide note. With older kids, the disinterested attitude can be deceiving. They act increasingly like they don't need you, but based on my experience, this is *exactly* the time for you to be more involved in their lives.

It's often said that kids don't come with a manual. The problem is that even if they did, we'd be focusing on the wrong part of parenting. We'd be looking at the *child's* development. We'd focus on infancy to toddler, then child to adolescent. We'd miss the oft-overlooked development of adult to parent.

I can't stress this enough to parents: I *understand* that you still want to have your Mommy time or your Dad's cave. Before you had kids, you probably didn't consider that you'd need a break from them to recharge your *you*. If someone told you, before you had kids, that simply going to the bathroom in peace is harder than swallowing an egg whole, you wouldn't have believed them.

Of course, you had no idea how much time being a parent would take. None of us did. Who could have known that something as simple as giving a twenty-two-inch person a bath could turn into a production? They've got their own tub, in which the water has got to be just so, the special Elmo watermelon-scented body wash, the special Big Bird shampoo, and you've only got twenty-four seconds to dry them off completely, missing no folds so as to avoid a rash, then you've got to wrap them up in their own cute little pink bunny towel with the ears on it that has to be laundered in Dreft on the gentle cycle. Meanwhile, when you're prepping for work in the morning, you've got it down to an Olympic sport—stop-watched at eighty-four seconds flat—to wash your body and hair, shave, dry, and get dressed.

Your naïveté is in the same dresser drawer as your high school ring and fake ID. You've replaced it with the maturity that comes from experiencing a life filled with baby formula, applications for summer programs, and homework that needs to be checked. Now you've got a schedule that would make the Obamas look like couch potatoes. You're juggling an eight-year-old with pneumonia, a project due at work, and a spouse who's traveling this week.

Do you remember when you didn't need a date night to be with the person you love? *Way* back when you could have sex before 11:00 p.m. Ah, those were the good ol' days. That was before the travel soccer league scheduled three practices plus a home and an away game each week; before you volunteered to coach your son's football team; before *every single weekend* was somebody's birthday. Now when you go shopping, you rush through the store so that you can be home in time to meet the piano teacher and relieve the sitter.

To parent is to sacrifice. But I don't need to remind you about that. What you probably do need to hear, though, is that to do it right, to be a good parent, there has to be balance. So go out with your friends. Talk on the phone for more than nine seconds without being asked something by somebody. Date. Do *you*. You have to. The trick is to do you enough to stay centered. So go get a massage—it's on me.

There's nothing wrong with still wanting to be an adult. As kids, that's all we ever dreamed of. You went to school, found the right job, and bought the right house so that you could be *that* kind of adult. I remember being at a drive-in movie—and I wanted to be *grown* so bad. I'd just seen *Smokey and the Bandit*. Burt Reynolds was so cool . . . and his car? *Dammnnn!* It was so powerful that even today I find myself fiendin' for a black Camaro Firebird. I remember leaving the movie in awe, asking my dad when I'd be able to drive. I wanted *out* of childhood more than anything.

Parents have to get comfortable with a little adult fun. Adults have to learn that too much adult fun makes you look like a kid. It's a question of credibility. You can't get your kids to see you as their parent when all that separates you from them is age. On the other hand, you can't get them to see you as human or relatable if you don't ever look like you're having fun. You both need space. You both need to explore you. You and your kids need balance.

There's an inherent balancing of desires against responsibilities that rumbles through every day of parenthood. The duality of a parent's existence makes Mommy go to bed dressed in a sexy negligee for Daddy and then don a plain old housecoat in time for their five-year-old son to creep into their bed at 3:24 a.m.

Schools need healthy parents. Kids need excuses removed. Both parents and kids need to understand that grown-ups are forever in pursuit of an internal balance—between being close enough to kids to help them but not so close that parents get caught up in acting like kids.

"I Have No Idea Where He Learned That . . . "

YOUR KIDS DON'T just look like you—they act like you. You accept this when they do something impressive. "My son is really good in math, just like I was." When they act up in class, though, it's somebody else's fault. "That's his *father's* side of the family coming out."

Day after day, principals and teachers have to listen to parents lie about how different they are from their child, how they were such hardworking students, thoroughly organized, always listening to their parents.

Educators know that parents are as messed up as their children. If a kid is lazy, we know that either the parents taught it to the child or they allowed it. Anne Ford, a friend, mentor, and longtime educator, once told me, "If you want to find a fool, follow one home." If there's a fool in your house, that fool has a child.

Yes, kids inevitably pick up their parents' worst habits, just as their parents did from their own parents. If you find yourself yelling at your kid, watch—in about five minutes, they will be in the next room yelling at their little sister. Curse in front of your four-year-old daughter, then wait for the phone call from the preschool informing you of how she's been dropping the F-bomb. Don't read much? Neither will your kids. Miss a lot of work, make excuses, have trouble getting along with others, overeat, drink, smoke? Well, wait and watch as your kids grow.

"Children are never good at listening to their elders," James Baldwin once said, "but they never fail to imitate them."

If you've learned anything from your upbringing, it should be that who you are is directly related to your interpretation of who your parents were. Consciously or unconsciously, you've internalized their best and worst characteristics. Whether you're running from it or to it, you cannot escape that you are your parents' child.

Parents Are like Cars

WHEN I WORK with parents, the first thing I have to do is make an assessment. I have to know, in broad terms, what *they* know. It's all too easy to get misled by what someone does for a living. In the real world, I've found that a person's profession is no indication of how effectively they parent. I've educated the children of principals and preachers, Ph.D.s and the unemployed. I've found that the best thing I can do is to take each parent as a parent.

Often, those kids who come from the most economically privileged homes present the most complex cocktail of issues. Well-to-do parents tend to engage in hyperparenting. They over-think everything. At the other end of the spectrum, I will meet a mother who hasn't worked in decades, is living in near squalor, but who has a terrific grasp of how to parent her child. My grandmother was fond of saying, "People is people." I'd amend that slightly: "Parents is people too."

Now I'm going to give you a chance to do what I do—assess. In general, I find that there are three types of parents. All three have something to offer their kids, and all face their own challenges. Once I know what kind of parent I'm working with, I can better support them and their children.

You and your kids can do this assessment together. When

I first meet with a family at Capital Prep, parents are sophisticated enough to put on a public persona that often overstates how effectively they parent. When they're in my office, they're more compassionate, have a greater handle on discipline and structure than they do in real life. In my office, they are all superb parents who read with their kids each night, check homework, set rigid bedtimes, create and keep schedules, don't drink, smoke, or fart.

The longer that I work with the family, the better I get to know them and, of course, the truth comes out. The students themselves are the first to offer a window on reality. Most kids aren't good at holding up a façade anyway. After hearing her mother recite an accomplished parenting résumé, the child will pipe up, "What? Mom, you never check my homework because you are *always* at work!" Awkward silence . . .

Take a little time. Do a self-assessment—and be honest with yourself. I can't help you to help your child if you're more concerned about how you look than the work we need to do together. It's one thing to start flossing your teeth two days before you go to the dentist. It's another to refuse the X-ray that will identify the cavities.

Open wide—let's take some X-rays.

WHAT KIND OF CAR ARE YOU?

1. My primary car has
   a. A spoiler and/or ground effects
   b. A flatbed
   c. At least one sliding door

2. My kids and I like/listen to essentially the same music

   a. Always

   b. Sometimes

   c. Never

3. If I'm late or miss my child's event, it is most likely because

   a. Our schedules conflicted

   b. I had to work

   c. I was at my other child's event

4. I borrow my teenager's clothes or shoes

   a. Always

   b. Sometimes

   c. Never

5. Last evening I

   a. Got tied up running errands

   b. Got tied up at work

   c. Got tied up with my kids' homework

6. In a typical three-month period, I go out socially, without my kids

   a. Two or more times

   b. Two or fewer times

   c. Never

7. I feel like my kids and I are friends

   a. Strongly agree

   b. Agree

   c. Disagree

8. In a week, I am scheduled to attend my kids' activities

   a. Two or fewer times

b. Two or more times

c. At least three times

9. When I go to the store, it's typically to buy groceries.

a. Disagree—I am as likely to be at the mall

b. Agree—but I do spend a good amount of time purchasing for work

c. Strongly agree—I only shop for myself when there is a special event

10. If my kids had to classify me as a car, they would call me a

a. Sports car

b. Pickup truck

c. Minivan

Tally the results to determine the predominant parenting strategy that you employ.

If most of your responses were choice *a*, you're a sports car parent. Sporty parents mainly drive a sporty car. Their cars have two doors. When you sit in them, it feels like you could reach out the window and touch the ground. A car seat? Naw, that would never fit in back. Spoilers, ground effects, and racing stripes all announce the arrival of sporty mom or dad. They blast the latest songs in their cute convertibles with their hair, hands, and feet perfectly polished. The extreme sporty mom can be seen driving with her left foot hanging out the window.

Sporty parents are fun, just not very responsible. They *forget*. Permission slips, games, pickup times all get a little scrambled in their *very busy* minds. Yeah, sporty parents are nothing if not busy. They'll pull up to the parent-principal meeting, screeching on two wheels, giving a big hello to the last parent who has politely waited with me and the sporty parent's son so the kid doesn't feel like such a loser. Their life is *so* hectic. Of course it is. When you're the most important person in your life, it can be a real challenge fitting in your kids. Don't get me wrong. All types of parents love their kids. Sporty parents just have a very complicated way of showing it.

Sporty parents have some great attributes. They teach their children to have fun and love life. Don't underestimate this. Too many grown people move dronelike through their day, constantly stressed out and miserable.

But sporty parents do have to work on being more considerate. It hurts their kids more than a child can typically express when their sporty parent misses something or is late. The parent's forgetfulness is seen as a sign of disregard. No child, and even fewer adults, can deal with being disregarded. So what a sporty parent most needs to work on is being there.

If most of your answers were choice *b*, then I'd consider you a work vehicle. You're an all-purpose pickup truck. Like it or not, you exist to work. Like sporty parents, worker parents are designed with very little space for children. Parents of this type are convinced that as long as they make enough money, they're good parents.

There's no particular profession that fills the ranks of such parents. I've seen parents of all stripes spend every waking moment going to or coming from work. They include nurse's assistants who work the third shift and investment bankers who put in seventy hours a week. They also include contractors who are always fixing up somebody else's house while their own kitchens display leaky faucets and bathrooms with falling-down tiles. I'd add to this group principals who write books, travel the country speaking, and appear in weekly broadcasts for CNN.

These work parents believe that parents are providers and that the best parents are the best providers. They believe that keeping a roof over their kids' heads supersedes going to ball games and hosting sleepovers. They believe that their kids *know* that they love them, even though they can't be there when their kids want them to be. These work parents are goal oriented. There's a position, or an investment, or a strategy they have to implement. If their kids could just bear with them . . .

Yes, it does hurt the child of a worker parent when he looks into the audience and sees an empty seat where his mom or dad should be. And for their part, worker parents aren't oblivious to their hurt. These parents don't feel so good when the first time they meet the principal is the day their kid graduates from high school.

You know the corporate catchphrase about striking a "work/life" balance? Being overtaxed at work is no excuse for not being there for your kids. It's not black-and-white—either stay home or go to work. It's about coming home a *bit* more. Balance is the worker parent's Achilles' heel. Sacrifice is their strength. What this type of parent needs to understand is that sometimes it's work that needs to be sacrificed.

Finally, if most of your answers were choice *c*, then you're a family-car parent. You're the type of parent whose identity is Parent. Parents with a capital "P" drive minivans and SUVs. Even if they're not stay-at-home moms or dads, their job is one that allows them to be around their kids almost all the time. Family-vehicle parents are regulars at their practices and parent-teacher organization (PTO) meetings. They're indefatigable carpoolers and facilitators of their kids' activities, and no time—outside of work—is spent without their children. These supercommitted family-vehicle types fill weekends and evenings with family activities. Girl Scouts, swimming, music lessons, softball, and soccer—they've got it covered.

Of course, family-vehicle types have issues with balance, too. They basically have no life outside of their kids. When their children tell them they want to go to the movies with their friends—rather than mom or dad—yes, their feelings get a little hurt. And no, sorry, it's not cool if they tag along but promise not to sit in the same row.

The family-vehicle parents' primary challenge is that they obsess over their kids. No one can tolerate nor does anyone deserve to be obsessed over. Kids need room—room to grow and make mistakes on their own.

Each of the three types of parents serves a purpose. But all struggle with balance issues. None will ever truly change. The job of all types is to find what is useful in their parenting style and learn from it. Sporty cars, find someone to teach your kids a work ethic. Work vehicles, try to lighten up. Family vehicles, develop some nonkid interests. In the end, all of you can parent within your own range of strengths and interests. Remember, you're all just people. You're allowed your imperfections. Yes, it's normal to be selfish even in this area of parenting—supposedly, the most selfless of endeavors.

Daddy's Kids

BUZZ BUZZ . . . He looks at me, and I at him. The ringing of the phone is a familiar interruption. An awkward moment. His big brown eyes both question and dare me to respond.

Buzz buzz . . . "It's *The Giving Tree,* Dad. This is *your* favorite book." I'm paralyzed. My reading slows in this puckered silent conversation between eyes, his and mine. The words, now committed to memory from years of reading, are hard to peel from the wide, sparse pages. *Buzz buzz* . . .

It's 9:15 p.m. I've just gotten home and my son Mason, eight, has waited up for me to read to him. He and Walker, five, have run my wife, Lalani, ragged—again. For yet another night she's wrestled, yelled, pleaded, and relented her way through homework, piano, soccer, bath, books, bed, and dinner.

I've still got my tie on, one button undone. The earpiece is still in my ear. My blazer and coat are still on, my hat tucked under my arm, as I balance on the edge of Mason's sports-themed comforter. In the distance, Lalani and Walker negotiate through the remainder of her patience and his overly tired little body.

Buzz buzz . . . Mason is patient but eight. As my right hand sneaks into the phone's holster like a gunslinger, I try to be inconspicuous.

"What if something is going on at the school?" I say to myself, rationalizing answering the call. "We've got a basketball game tonight and a few kids in Maryland on a college overnight." Finally, "What if somebody didn't make it home?" My hand pushes down, pokes my BlackBerry's belly button, and answers. I hope he understands, again. "I'm just gonna answer it and then I'll finish reading," I promise. I could throw this damn thing against the wall and applaud as it splashes into a million goddamned pieces. I can hear my wife in Walker's room stop reading, exasperated, listening to me negotiate the right to answer that goddamned phone, again. I shake my head. Like I need her to remind me.

Deep down I worry that my sons are going to resent me in the same way I spent my entire life resenting my father. He missed everything: from games to graduation, from girls to the gift of a call on my birthday. He, too, was preoccupied with his life, *important things,* other people. How could he? How could he miss it all? Where was he? What could I have done to make him not want to be there for me, with me? All I wanted was for him to be there. I could have gotten past the fact that he blackened my mother's eyes. I could've forgiven him for living with his new family, but tonight, any night but tonight with this goddamned BlackBerry, I need him there, here, to tell me what to do.

I opened a school because I'd seen too many kids blame themselves for their father's absence. I'd watched too many girls date the wrong dudes and too many boys grow up to become the wrong dudes. I came to do it differently. I was gonna show these sorry-ass men who put everybody else before their kids that their kids didn't need them, because they had me as their principal. Then I was blessed with the school, sons, and a wife. I was a principal, father, and husband, in that order, on the goddamned cell again, worried about somebody else's kids, forfeiting another precious moment with mine, disappointing my wife and myself. I try convincing myself that I'm truly doing the right thing, making the right decision, yet I feel like crap. I hope Mason understands that I've got to answer this phone for just a second. *I'm sorry,* an inner voice says. *Really sorry.*

I inhale. "Hello . . ." I listen for a few moments. "I'll be right there" rolls out of my mouth like a casual breath. A student, abandoned at school, has no ride home. So I button that button, fix my tie, and cock my legs on the floor. Mason doesn't understand.

God, I hate this cell phone, this call, this calling, the duplicity. I hate the fact that this doesn't make any sense. I wish my sons could see me staring at them when they sleep, frozen by the stillness of their cherub cheeks. Watching them sleep pulls a smile out of the stones of my face on the worst days. Stories of their foibles entertain my staff. Anticipation of the day I drop them off at college forced me into financial discipline before they were potty trained. My boys and I talk about how they'll treat their wives, how many kids they're gonna have, what kind of houses they'll live in. I'm hard on them so that I'll be able to spoil instead of raise my grandkids. Tonight? I gotta go back to work.

I would carve the sun into finger food for my two little boys. Tonight, I have to go back to work because some other dad is asleep on his responsibility. I rush to and through the book's thoughtful end. Pray at full speed, "God bless Mommy and Daddy . . .," snatch the lights off, creep out of his room, and slither down the stairs as my wife rhetorically offers, "Leaving?" To which I assure,

"For a minute." My school is a half hour from the house—at 75 mph. It's 9:30 now and we haven't spoken in person since yesterday night at 9:30. Tonight, I haven't even seen her. I kissed her before I left at 4:45 a.m. She didn't budge.

As I sneak out, the house alarm punctuates my departure with a staccato, *Front door open!* I unplug my car door, stuff myself back into the still-warm driver's seat, and look up to see that Mason has gotten out of the hurriedly tucked bed that I left him in. He's positioned in his window, folding the book under his arms. I wave and smile. He doesn't. He watches me back out. I smile again. He doesn't. Maybe he doesn't see me. It's dark.

Lemonade

OUR SCHOOLS DIDN'T get this bad by themselves. Parents from all classes are sending pampered kids who are intentionally insulated from adversity. These parents are afraid their nine-year-old child will be scarred for life because she wasn't invited to a classmate's birthday party. These maladjusted, overly dramatic parents have flooded our schools with kids who cower in the corner as a first option. America has got to raise tougher kids because there's an army of toughies who have invaded our shores, guided by their own manifest destiny.

Children from all over the world have arrived at our neighborhood schools and, without even being fluent in English, are commandeering all of the education that they can. These kids get it. They approach the battle for economic supremacy with a sniper's precision. They are efficient. They don't waste a lot of time on whining. They get to class on time, come with their homework done, and keep it moving.

Their parents don't come in and advocate. If the teacher said that the child was wrong, that's it. They were wrong, apologize, and change the behavior. Spend a little time with these modest hardworking families and it makes sense why they do well in school and life. Who wouldn't want to accept them into college, give them a scholarship, or give them a job? They are freakin' machines.

They didn't come here to fool around. They want an American education. In their eyes, this is real education. They understand the boundless possibilities that even an average American education has to offer. While we look at what our schools are lacking, they are scouring the floor for our scraps so that they can turn them into a meal to feed generations.

Education is a means to an end, the fulfillment of a dream—period. Knock immigrant kids all you want—and while you do that, they'll just become the valedictorian of your son's senior class. Successful students know how to play the game; they don't let the game play them.

A successful student doesn't necessarily need highly driven and committed parents. Stop beating yourself up every time your kid brings home a C. The parents of some of my very best kids at Capital Prep simply send their kids to school and never attend parent-teacher organization (PTO) meetings, let alone return a phone call from the school. They miss just as many games as the struggling kids' parents. If these kids are lucky, their parents *might* come to graduation. No, it's not ideal, and I wouldn't recommend it, but it is a reality for many kids.

It's often tough for me to help parents understand their role in their child's success. I've seen parents who to all outward appearances seem perfect give birth to Lucifer, Beelzebub, or one of the fallen angels. These parents look like the total package—good educations, thriving careers, well-ordered lives—but, for whatever reason, their style of parenting is the wrong fit for that child. Maybe their child needs *less* attention, not more. Less freedom and more direction. The problem is that none of us knows this until the water is out of the cup.

The immigrant parents are working those proverbial nineteen jobs, stuck at a strip mall behind a white mask in the haze of acetone scraping some other mother's hard, ashy feet while their kids try to study in the back by the row of foot massagers. Is this the ideal situation for learning? I don't know, but it's damn sure working. These same kids are beating affluent suburban Americans in top prep schools—astonishing when you consider that they didn't even speak the English language a few years ago.

Look, I'm a functionalist. In my mind, if it works, it's right.

What I see in all successful parent-child relationships is humility and respect. These kids know that they are kids. They never think that the sun rises and sets on them. They genuinely grasp that they have a greater responsibility to someone other than their own very active id. They have chores—yes, old-school *chores*, remember them? Some are traditional, menial jobs like sweeping, dusting, or taking out the trash, or more high-end ones like after-school volunteering. Chores are not some corny relic from the *Leave It to Beaver* era. Having daily or weekly chores forces kids to face up to life's facts, makes them realize that they have to pay *something* for the place they are taking up.

Good kids are neither Black nor White, rich nor poor, inner-city nor suburban. They're just good. We all know who they are. Some get top grades and others don't. Good kids are almost universally liked by adults, respected by their classmates. Without seeming to work at it, they make their parents look like geniuses, lucky bastards, or both.

I'm convinced that, from the middle class up, we give our kids too damn much. You can do your own headcount: How many schoolkids do you personally know without an Xbox, PlayStation, or Wii? Without an iPod, iPhone, or iPad? Who could blame our kids for not having a work ethic? They don't have to make their own friends at the playground these days: moms have got them networking online, arranging "play dates"—but that's even something of a misnomer. Unlike generations before, we don't even let our kids go out and play. Child-to-child conflicts are refereed by adults. We're all on pins and needles about bullying and then we wonder why our kids disengage from the real world, withdraw into an online cocoon, forming a private universe of cyber-relationships.

Whether it's elementary school kids or teenagers, mostly they only go outside when they walk from the front door to your SUV, where more often than not they stop conversing with you altogether, turning on the pacifier of the backseat DVD player or PlayStation while balancing the texting weapon of choice, iPhone, Droid, or the aptly nicknamed *Crack*Berry. Our generation of parents has sucked the simplicity out of even car rides. Punch buggy, anyone? Not unless it's an iPhone app.

Not all success makes sense. It's not always linear. In many cases, successful kids in our schools succeed for no reason more complicated than they have the desire to succeed. They don't come to school with any overwhelming advantages. Many are living in cramped apartments with eight family members, three generations deep. Some come from places—like Darfur—that make South Central Los Angeles look like Club Med. Still they succeed. They succeed in school and life because they understand and manifest the word *will*—both verb and noun. Over and over, they tell themselves they *will* succeed. And, equally important, they exhibit the *will* to succeed. They don't waste breath complaining about what they don't have. Successful kids know what they don't have and are focused on overcoming their limitations.

Don't let your kids get caught in the self-victimizing trap, thinking that everybody else has it better than them. Every family has precisely what it has and yours is no different. Who gives a damn about the Joneses unless you are a Jones? The parents of your kids' friends have issues just like your family does. Don't let your kids trick you into thinking that they don't.

The kids at their school come from homes that are headed by single mothers, married couples, gay and straight parents who are in the process of breaking up or fighting to stay together. That's their business. Tell your kids to mind their own damn business, go do their homework, and hope they don't wake up tomorrow with a zit the size of a cherry tomato under their eye.

Over and over what I've observed is that successful students' parents don't do the studying for their kids, even if they do it together. These parents don't come to school to take their tests for their kids.

Successful kids come from every country and nationality, from all varieties of parenting styles. What separates them is their decision making. Kids who do the best know when to say when. They don't buckle to peer pressure. They know when shoplifting a candy bar has crossed the line into out-and-out robbery. They're just as curious as the other kids. Yeah, they peek into their parents' liquor cabinet, crack open the vodka, and refill it with tap water. They just don't down the whole bottle and then blame it on their uncle. Sure, they have friends over when their parents are out of town, but they don't turn the house into a free-for-all that would make the cast of *Animal House* blush.

Successful kids are not perfect. In fact, I've seen far too many *perfect* kids implode. The self-destruction can be triggered by a few bad grades, a breakup, or something as simple as a misunderstood e-mail. These are the kids who cheat on exams because they are so connected to the façade of perfection that they'll do anything to get ahead. When working out and eating right isn't enough, they develop bulimia. Perfect kids think that they are smarter than the teacher. These kids find fault in the entire world and when fault appears in them, they have a meltdown, trying desperately to erase it. No joke—perfect kids are a danger to themselves.

Successful kids make *mostly* right decisions. They don't disrespect the teacher and they don't get thrown out of class. They haven't heard a single rumor worth fighting over, nor have they seen an iPod that they'd disgrace their family to steal. They keep their head down, their mouth shut, and get an education while the cool kids make fun of their clothes.

But don't get it twisted: Successful kids *ain't no punks.* They're not sorry-ass whiners, focused on the half-empty dirty glass that their life is served in. They know that this is the show. No more rehearsals. While the spoiled kids wallow in what is missing, the successful kids are out finding it.

Every school has an education in it. Despite what you may hear in the media, even America's most violent and oppressive schools do send kids to college. The withered-up lemon in the back corner of your fridge may have lost its tang—but it's still a lemon. You can still squeeze a few drops of juice from it.

A generation ago, parents taught their kids to make lemonade. The kids took out a card table and a few folding chairs; mixed up some lemon juice, sugar, and water; made a sign with cardboard and a magic marker; and hawked ice-cold glasses to neighbors for a few quarters. Imagine that: a lemonade stand in 2011.

In that simple act, these parents would send their children into their teens with a foundation, a work ethic, and, at its core, an essential life lesson: take something simple and put a smile on someone's day.

Today's parents would never dream of leaving their children to fend for themselves at a lemonade stand. They'll go buy the Minute Maid lemonade premixed at the supermarket, then have the kids pass it out in Spiderman cups at their *vintage*-themed birthday party. Complete the scene with pony rides and the updated version of the *Little Rascals* playing on the 110-inch projection screen in the backyard.

You know that kid in the goofy glasses who couldn't make it to the party? He couldn't come because he works every Saturday sweeping his uncle's barbershop—and when you hear about it, you're ready to call the Department of Children and Family Services. But that's why your kid is likely to work for the barbershop kid in twenty years.

Listen, even *slim* odds are better than none. Until grown folks can get some good sense and fully correct the sins of public education, this is all that we have to give our kids. There is no other option. Teach them to make the best of it. Teach them to make lemonade.

Audit Your Home!

CONDUCT AN EDUCATIONAL audit of your home—*today*. Start with the physical space. Where do your children do their homework? Is it quiet, clear, and free of clutter? If not, it needs to be. I don't care if you live in a palace or a tenement, your children cannot effectively study in a mess. Clean up! Remove distractions from their workspace.

Create a *shrine* to learning. Education is like religion: it's a complete lifestyle. Students and practicing Buddhists can be identified by what they do with their time and space. College kids live in dorms, study in libraries, dress, act, and talk about getting an education. Until your children get to college, they live with you, so you have to immerse them in the lifestyle of education. Make your home a campus, an academic temple.

What are you spending your money on? Are there more DVDs and video games than *books* in your house? When you spend thousands of dollars on a home theater or a game room filled with hours of distractions, you better believe that your kids are paying attention. That misplaced sense of values—and valuable resources—could cost you dearly down the road. People always want me to tell them how to get money to defray the cost of college. They want to know about scholarships and investment strategies. My answer is simple: "Invest your money in books for your babies, chief."

Smart kids with high test scores are made, not born, and these are the kids who tend to get the most money for college. Build smart kids in their crib by filling it with books and educational toys to hard-wire them for intellectual growth. Don't waste money on games to keep toddlers quiet, because, ironically, when they start school, they're likely to be the noisiest kids in the classroom. The more access kids have to academic materials when they're young, the better behaved they are when they come to school.

Americans are under the illusion that we are *born* smart. While the rest of the world spend their lives scrimping to earn a vote in the international meritocracy, we accept the fallacy of heredity.

When our houses aren't focused on education, is it any surprise that our kids aren't either? If the only books our children have in their home are those on loan from their school, then our kids are getting the implicit message that we as parents don't value education. Xbox and PlayStation games, the latest DVDs and iTunes cost good money, yet this country is full of libraries that lend books for free or often sell off nearly brand-new hardcovers for fifty cents or a buck. Drop by your nearest library this week. Get your kids some free books.

Your kids need to *learn* the art of learning in an academic setting. This includes the discipline of maintaining focus through an active and, at times, difficult task. Sure, there are valuable educational programs on television and informational DVDs on the market. But watching TV and movies and listening to music are passive and can't take the place of actively *working*. Rather, kids must roll up their sleeves to start—and more important, *finish*—

reading a book, writing a composition, or even completing a Su-doku or crossword puzzle.

Continue the audit of your home by counting what your family does with its time. High schoolers preparing for college should be spending at least two to three hours a night in uninterrupted study. Your child can't complete a full school day's work in a forty-five-minute study hall. If he can, you need to talk to the school.

Every school night, she should have homework. If she tells you she doesn't, she's probably lying or her teachers are asleep at the wheel. That means the "auditor" eye has to peer into the classroom. No excuses. Call or e-mail the teachers: you've got to find out why there's no homework in your child's book bag. A true audit doesn't stop at the first answer. If it sounds crazy, then it probably is. Find the solution when the answer is insufficient.

As for technology, you've got to be real with yourself. How long do you leave your kids alone on the computer? In a few seconds, they can google some of the meanest words, and nastiest images, you've ever seen. I've got a simple fix: don't leave your kids alone on the computer. If you're not literally over their shoulder, simply audit their computer use by checking the history of their Internet searches and the cache of chats and e-mails. And don't fall for that specious argument about "invasion of privacy." If your children want privacy, tell them to grow up and buy a house. The Web is a powerful educational tool, but it's also a minefield of distractions and potential interpersonal conflicts. Our kids—especially our teenagers—cannot be left on the computer without you checking in at fifteen-minute intervals.

As a principal of an urban school, I can tell you that these days the majority of schoolyard beefs start online—long after the final bell has rung. We've raised a generation of Internet gangsters who spend more time blasting off on each other than they do studying. And it's really not that complicated: most kids fail in class because they *fail* to do homework. Instead of studying, too many of our kids spend half the night online worrying about who hates who. You thought they were online researching that social studies assignment, but, no, they were too busy talking smack on Facebook and Twitter.

The last part of our home audit involves you—the parent. Do *you* read? If so, how often? Take a moment to notice exactly where you are when your kids are doing homework. Are you close by in case your son needs help? Are you sending the right verbal (and nonverbal) cues, letting him know that you think homework is important enough to turn off the ball game, get off that *goddamn* BlackBerry, and stop whatever you're doing to help?

All of us parents know that kids don't respond well to "Do as I say, not as I do." But they do respond to your setting a supportive example. Telling a child to go off and struggle with something—whether it's algebra or Shakespeare—that they simply don't understand is irresponsible. Stay close. Read over your daughter's shoulder. Struggle with her—and you'll be well on your way to establishing the foundation of a strong community, which is a home that supports education.

Now I'm gonna talk to your kids for a minute. I'll tell them what so many parents wish they could say. I *might* hit them a little harder than you would, but that's why you buy a book like mine. I push the envelope so you won't have to.

More Than They Can Handle:
A Note to Your Teenager

Look, kids, your parents are in over their heads. They need your help. They don't have the strength to deal with one smart-mouthed kid, let alone two or three. So stop. Please. Tell your brother and sister to stop, too. As a matter of fact, let's call today a "jerk-free" holiday.

Sometimes your parents are holding on for dear life. They can't have you complicating things. Day after day, you point out their limits, their inconsistencies, their insecurities. C'mon, chief, you know that hurts. They're your parents. They're not superhuman. Cut 'em a break. They do mean well.

Your parents find themselves challenged in dealing with your stuff *and* theirs. So although they have always—and will always—love you, *liking* you when you're a brat can really be a chore.

You need to understand what they are dealing with before you can put their reactions into perspective. And you need this perspective so that you can get on with your life. You can't take their reactions to you too personally. You will carry them through life like a backpack full of rocks—aching and rubbing you raw. You don't need that baggage. Parenting is trial and error. Even a great chef has burned a main course. Don't let the smoke and the charred edges fool you—your parents can still cook.

Your parents do what they do because of who they are. They would treat any child who has come to them with your gifts and challenges the way they treat you. Yeah, you're right, sometimes they do treat your siblings differently. You'd be the first to admit that you are all different and that's the only way you treat different people—even when they all came from the same womb.

This is the only way they know to express their love, fear, joy, resentment, and hope. They are still coming out of the smoke that was the inferno of their own childhood. Clarity is miles down the road, far from where they are right now. Their reactions to you are three parts guesswork, two tablespoons of advice, and a smidge of experience. Taste that, tell me what's missing. . . .

Parenting is taking all of their time and concentration. At times it's like doing the Electric Slide across a tightrope. Help them out, chief. Pick something up. Wash something. Surprise them and don't talk back. Why? You're right, it doesn't always make sense. Congrats, Detective Stabler— you caught them. Now what? How about we call it even this time and you act like you love them? I promise in about fifteen years you'll be in a room staring at a version of you, talking like a version of your folks. Guess what? You're going to call them up for advice and you will both appreciate each other that much more.

They want to figure it out. Your parents want to do right by you. They want to prove their parents wrong. Please, please, *please*—be patient with them. They'll start figuring things out in time to drop you off at college. Then when you get back, they'll be ready to advise you on your career and family.

Typically, parents are able to focus on you and your needs. Okay, it's true—there are times when they aren't. See, the problem is that they are parents all the time. A physician works in shifts. A pilot lands the jet and has some downtime in his hotel. Professional athletes get an off-season. There is no downtime, no off-season, from parenting.

When Dad's had a hard day at work or an argument with your mother, he's still your father. When Mom's just been laid off, or tells you she's met a new guy, she's still your mother. As they battle weight gain and struggle with childhood trauma, they are still parents. Your parents. There is no respite. Ever. Even a vacation ain't a vacation from being a parent.

Your parents are going to stumble and fall. They aren't looking for sympathy; a little compassion, maybe fewer headaches would help, but they think they've got this. Just don't add anything.

Your parents give you as much love as they have to give. No love is unconditional, nor should it be. All love is limited by the ability of one to love and the object of their affection to inspire love. You should have to work to impress them. You shouldn't be able to do whatever the hell you want and expect that they'll love it.

I see parents all the time, and many of them damn sure have some conditions on their love. One father once told me that if he knew his daughter was going to come to the U.S. and underachieve, he'd have left her back home in Mexico. Say what you want, but it makes sense. You are their greatest investment. More than any 401(k), you ensure them a comfortable retirement. So when you get here and only cost them, that makes you a bad investment.

No faith is blind. All faith can see. Their faith in you accepts the wrong that you do; it doesn't make them blind to it. They accept it because deep down they know who they are and who they've been.

Sure, they're flawed. Guess what? They're human. They should be disappointed when you disappoint them. We have the highest expectations for the people we love the most. Deal with it. Take the high expectations that come with the greatest kind of love.

PART FIVE

Gatekeepers

Teachers' Unions: The Worst Thing That Ever Happened to Education

THE LEADERS OF OUR teachers' unions have ruined public schools. They are the ones who created the school calendar that is too short and a six-and-a-half-hour school day, and who've made firing ineffective teachers almost impossible.

Teachers' unions are not the only professional parasites feasting on our public schools. Add the unions representing principals, secretaries, custodians, security officers, and paraprofessionals and you'll begin to see why our schools don't work. All these groups exist to improve adult working conditions rather than the end product of public education—students. They've been profoundly successful. Their working conditions are awesome. Our schools are failing.

I am in a union. *Yes,* I am a card-carrying, dues-paying member of the Hartford Federation of Teachers. *No,* I don't want to be in this union. *No,* I don't support their efforts to maintain the employment of principals whose schools were closed for failure to educate. What I believe hardly matters. The money that comes out of my check every two weeks pays the union's president and its attorneys to ensure that failed principals get to keep their jobs.

No, I don't want my money being used to support candidates and causes that, if they prevail, will simply maintain the status quo of public education. That doesn't matter, because the dues are deducted from my pay automatically. Sure, I can "get out" of the union. All that means is that I'll forfeit my right to vote in the union. I'll still have to pay what is referred to as an "agency fee" or "fair share" of the fees to the attorneys whom the union selects to negotiate a contract that I don't support. This is the law in states throughout America.

Many public employees *must* be in a union or pay as a non-member. I'm the principal of a public school. I'm a public employee, so I must pay an organization to which I'm diametrically, ethically, and personally opposed.

We, the employees of public schools, have the best work calendar of all full-time professionals. Most of us work no more than 187 days a year versus a typical 250 days for the rest of the economy. Our workday is 6½ hours versus 8 hours, or 32½ hours a week. Compared to a typical 40-hour workweek, teachers work one less day per week than most full-time professionals and—let me clue you in on a little secret—our salaries are *not* nearly as low as they're often portrayed. For example, the average teacher salary in Hartford in 2011, one of the poorest and lowest-performing districts in Connecticut, is $70,000. According to the United States Bureau of Labor Statistics 2010 data, the mean teacher's salary nationally is $55,990—compared to the national mean of $44,410 for full-time employees. So how do we explain the pervasive belief that teachers are grossly underpaid?

This belief is based on the 1960s pre-union salaries of female teachers, many of whom taught in poorly funded Catholic schools. It's also based on today's *starting* salaries—meaning those of twenty-one-year-old fresh-out-of-college *kids*. When compared to the salaries of other twenty-one-year-olds, new to the workforce and forced to live at home or with roommates, teachers' salaries are higher—especially when you consider that other recent college grads will work through the summer and all members of educators' unions will not. Then there are the benefits that educators reap.

Employees of public schools have the best benefits of all employees, public or private. My wife works for the headquarters of a major insurance company here in Connecticut. Still, my benefits as a public school employee are more generous than hers. We have great dental and medical coverage—doctors' offices call our insurance card the gold card. In fact, until a few years ago if any member of our union wanted, they could opt to get a sex-change operation or Lasik surgery and it too would be fully covered by our taxpayer-funded health insurance plan.

For all that the community provides us educators, as taxpayers you should expect more. Instead, there is no escaping the fact that our public school system is the most expensive failure in the industrialized world.

Education unions' leadership has convinced policy makers, concerned citizens, and parents that their members are underpaid, overworked, and underappreciated. No labor group has done a better job of portraying themselves as victims. I've always been impressed by how educator unions are able to portray master's degreed, white-collar intellectuals as suffering the conditions of blue-collar, disadvantaged laborers. I can't help but smile when I think of how effectively the teachers' unions have promulgated the myth that they feel *your pain.* Sure they feel it—they're the ones swinging the hammer. It's marketing genius. Middle-class people, most of whom live in the suburbs and are White, with summer homes *and* the time to use them, are being portrayed as downtrodden laborers being done wrong by "The Man"? Damn! I've got to give props for that.

It doesn't matter that research clearly shows that children from *all* types of schools lose as much as two and a half months of material over the summer. The unions continue to negotiate for *their* members to have the summers off. It doesn't matter that summer learning loss occurs in subject areas in which our kids need the most support, such as math and science. And it doesn't matter that summer learning loss affects minority and poor students most. Nope, educators' unions still demand that *their* members have the summers off.

The teachers' unions have made it virtually impossible to extend the school year. Across Connecticut, boards of education have to fight to add a day to the work year, let alone weeks. Were students to go to school for just six of the summer's ten weeks from the end of their freshman year through their senior year, they'd receive an additional *year* of instruction. Imagine. In the same four-year span of high school, each American teenager would receive five years' worth of education.

The leaders of the teachers' unions have flattened the expectations communities have for our children. So now, even when a school has a 71 percent dropout rate, the community won't demand the school's closure because we've accepted that teachers are underpaid and overworked. Because we don't expect much from our public schools, we easily accept that the school's failure must be the fault of the kids, poverty, race, this generation of parents, and standardized tests. These union leaders are disgraceful and must be brought to justice for what they've consciously done to the public trust, the public schools, the nation's future, and the communities' children.

OF COURSE, AS THE principal of a school whose theme is social justice, I can't negate the invaluable contributions made by trade unions in the nineteenth and twentieth centuries. A. Philip Randolph, leader of the Brotherhood of Sleeping Car Porters, conceived the 1964 March on Washington and stands alongside Martin Luther King Jr. and Rosa Parks in the pantheon of civil rights trailblazers. In fact, Dr. King was killed in Memphis during what was essentially a labor dispute among trash collectors. Millions of Jewish and Italian Americans know that their grandparents were protected from exploitation in sweatshops and inhumane working conditions by the Ladies' Garment Workers' Union. And for Hispanic Americans, few leaders are more revered than César Chávez for his decades-long crusade to improve working conditions of migrant farmworkers.

This conversation is about educated, privileged, and protected teachers whose schools cost too much and produce too little. The teachers' union leaders occupy the other side in the civil rights saga. They're the defenders of the status quo—the defiant defenders of inhumane conditions heaped on children, the least powerful among us. The outspoken Randi Weingarten, president of the American Federation of Teachers and the lesser-known

Dennis Van Roekel of the National Education Association are the Bull Connor and the Strom Thurmond of this civil rights epic.

Even as we laud Big Labor's role in combating racism, sexism, and fighting for a living wage, we must also remember an uglier legacy of the trade union movement: the corruption represented by Jimmy Hoffa and the Mafia takeover of the Teamsters. Obviously, I'm not saying that the two national teachers' unions are *par legal* in the pocket of La Cosa Nostra, but there's no denying that they embody the ruthlessness and Machiavellian tactics of white-collar mobsters.

In the 2010 hit documentary *Waiting for Superman,* one of the country's leading liberal journalists, *Newsweek*'s Jonathan Alter, nailed it right on the head. "It's very, very important to hold two contradictory ideas in your head at the same time," Alter said in the film. "Teachers are great—a national treasure. Teachers' unions are, generally speaking, a menace and an impediment to reform."

As Alter explains, the origins of the teachers' unions lie in a noble struggle: back when teaching was seen exclusively as "women's work" and women were still second-class citizens, underpaid and often exploited. However, in their current incarnations, the American Federation of Teachers and the National Education Association have indeed come to resemble the Brotherhood of Teamsters under Jimmy Hoffa: an all-powerful political juggernaut, more concerned with the absolute unconditional protection of dues-paying members—regardless of competence—than with the protection of their most vulnerable charges, the students of America.

For decades, the only people who told the story of the negative impact that unions have on education were conservatives. The trouble with the message of teacher accountability was the messenger. The general public simply didn't trust that voices from the political right could possibly be concerned about *all* children. Their statements attacking teachers' unions seemed only to betray a long-standing conservative—and arguably classist—political position against *all* organized labor.

For liberals and reformers, speaking out against the teachers' unions was, until very recently, considered utterly blasphemous. Those who were concerned about educational quality bought the idea that simply *because* someone had decided to be a teacher, that person was good. Calling out the extreme excesses of the teachers' unions was like badmouthing your own mother. Our country so values the *idea* of teachers that even as our schools fail to educate our children, we cannot bring ourselves to truly hold educators accountable for their failure to teach. Instead we blame ourselves, poverty, race, single parenthood, and our children for the lack of learning.

I throw my heart into the accountability discussion because I've witnessed the ugly truth. The teachers' union leadership for the past generation has actively fought every form of educational reform, both large and small. School choice through magnets, charters, privatization, or vouchers? No, no, no, and *hell* no. Tying students' performance to teachers' evaluations? Nope. Expanding programs such as Teach for America and New Leaders for New Schools that will make it easier for other professionals to become a teacher and/or school leaders? *No chance . . .* Rethinking the school calendar and working day? Okay, we'll talk—but how deep are your pockets?

It doesn't matter how much success these and other reform efforts have had in improving both teachers and learning, teachers' unions convulse and doggedly fight progress. No, all the efforts have not produced overwhelming success; however, reform efforts have led to the only educational progress in generations.

The education unions are simply not in the business of supporting teaching and learning. Their single preoccupation is apparently to leave no teacher behind.

Even the slightest suggestion that a policy or legislation will make it a bit easier to fire an incompetent teacher is fought vehemently by the teachers' unions. One scene in *Waiting for Superman*—a scene that drew audible gasps in the theater when I first saw it—reports that while 1 in 52 doctors loses his or her license for malpractice, only 1 in 2,500 teachers loses his or hers. After college, medical school, and residency, can medical doctors be that much worse at their jobs than the teachers who trained them?

I've watched union leaders intimidate young teachers who try to use their duty-free lunch to tutor kids. The same happens when a teacher volunteers to stay after school. The contract says that teachers are to be paid a rate that is commensurate with their hourly rate, which is based on years of service and education, not performance. Following the letter of the contract, if there is no money to pay the teacher, security officer, and custodians to be at the eighth-grade dance, there can be no eighth-grade dance. These iron-clad contracts, often backed by law, remove civility and decency from schools.

Time and again, teachers' unions fervently fight to keep low-performing teachers in the classroom and low-performing schools open. Like Philadelphia lawyers, they're trained to spot loopholes and technicalities. Their focus is not on the guilt or innocence of a union member, but on identifying how well the administrator followed the procedures. Teachers' unions primarily spend their money on three main goals: (1) negotiating working conditions through contracts with the municipalities; (2) defending teachers who have been reprimanded/negatively evaluated, and (3) supporting political candidates and legislation that will make it easier for them to do (1) and (2).

In my first year as principal of Capital Prep—for almost the full school year, in fact—I fought to remove a teacher whom I observed openly sleeping in class. Not once but twice. As the principal, it should have been really simple, right? He was asleep sitting in front of a class full of kids. I saw him both times—this is academic, right? Wrong.

I should have been able to call the teacher into my office. Like at any other job in America—from a construction worker to an investment banker—this should have been a straightforward conversation. "Look, you were sleeping on the job!" Then we should have been able to talk about how we could part ways and, perhaps, how he could one day teach again. Not so fast, Mr. First-Year Principal. Here comes the almighty union to protect its dues-paying member. Here comes the almighty teachers' union to protect the job of a teacher who is so unprofessional that he sleeps in class.

I fought with the Hartford Federation of Teachers every damn day for an entire school year, trying to get this guy off the job. Remember, this wasn't a case of hearsay: I personally saw him asleep in a class full of children. But that didn't matter. All the union was concerned about was the process I'd used. And, of course, since I was a first-year principal, there were some areas of process where I wasn't as sharp as a thirty-year union veteran.

The union simultaneously executed a strategy wherein they created diversions, such as physician's notes—as if "laziness" was a valid medical explanation—and media attacks. The Hartford Federation of Teachers tried to smear me personally with the local NBC and ABC affiliates—all to save a teacher with poor judgment who slept in class. What in the hell did I do wrong? His ass was asleep in a class full of kids! Why would they even want that guy in their union? Were his dues worth their reputation and the futures of those kids in that class?

They tried to make me assign him a mentor. A *freaking* mentor? For *sleeping*?

Then they said I had to counsel him and consider the stress of teaching. And my naïve, first-year principal's response was to shout the obvious: "But he was asleep! I saw it! Twice!"

During the investigation, his students and even his co-teacher wrote statements confirming that he'd slept in class on several other occasions. When the academic year was over, what had the local teachers' union achieved? They'd exhausted all legal avenues and had attacked me in the media for trying to remove a sleeping, ineffective tenured teacher. They went at me tooth and nail because I had the audacity to argue the *unthinkable:* that a teacher should be awake when he's in a classroom filled with children. By the time the teacher was finally removed from my school, our staff was fractured. Children and parents had been dragged into the fight, and the entire school was polarized. It took one more year to settle down the staff.

A few years later, I had a teacher leave a group of kids unsupervised in downtown Hartford until 9:00 p.m. while she went Christmas shopping at Walmart. When I confronted her, she nonchalantly replied, "They had my cell if there was a problem." It took seven months to get her removed from the classroom.

Understand: the sleeping teacher and the Christmas shopper were not *fired*. They were simply transferred. They could still find well-paying teaching jobs in the district. Yes, that's the power of a union.

ONE OF THE MORE disturbing scenes in *Waiting for Superman* depicts the transfer of incompetent teaching staff from one school to another, a process known as the "Dance of the Lemons" or the "Turkey Trot." Everyone familiar with the public school system across the country knows about this educational travesty. It's an unwritten pact between public school principals to pass around the lousiest tenured teachers. The thought is, "I can't fire them, so let's pass around the bad eggs," hoping—against all logic— that "I'll end up with a couple of teachers who are *less* lousy than the ones I was stuck with last semester."

In an interview I did for CNN's "Perry's Principles," I sat down with *Superman* director Davis Guggenheim and producer Lesley Chilcott. We talked about the Dance of the Lemons. Far from being a dirty little secret, the process of shifting ineffective teachers is "central" to public education's failing.

Joel Klein, the former chancellor of New York City's public schools, agrees. According to Klein, the heads of teachers' unions have created a contentious professional environment in which collegiality is forfeited for mindless skirmishes that waste hundreds of thousands of dollars and countless working hours defending something as trivial—and as unrelated to the welfare of students—as teachers' *right* to wear blue jeans to work. This isn't hyperbole! The Hartford Federation of Teachers went to a hearing, during a school year in which only 29 percent of the students graduated, fighting for the right of teachers to wear jeans, even though the kids they were teaching were required to wear uniforms. The HFT prevailed. Klein told me that New Yorkers were spending upward of $130 million per year on ineffective teachers who'd been placed in reassignment centers, the infamous "rubber rooms."

Filming another "Perry's Principles" for CNN, I interviewed David Suker, a teacher who'd been removed from the classroom. When we met, he hadn't taught in a New York City public school in eighteen months, during which time he still received his full $80,000 salary and benefits and was accumulating years toward his retirement.

Suker admitted to me that he'd "gone a little too far" when he blew up at a sixteen-year-old girl in his adult education class. After yelling at her, Suker said that he took her test and threw it in the trash, forcing her to dig through the trash bin in front of her classmates to retrieve it. Suker was written up and suspended from his teaching duties. He produced evidence of his multiple reprimands for "going too far." Yes, he'd gone too far, he acknowledged, yet he claimed that "the real reason" he was in the rubber room was because he'd uncovered that his principal was having an affair. Suker produced no evidence to substantiate his claim against the principal.

Most good teachers don't want anything to do with teachers' unions. As Alter says in *Superman,* there's a distinction between rank-and-file teachers and their egotistical leaders. Thousands of decent teachers around the country are getting *played* by their unions. The leaders are so deft at manipulation that they can make even thoughtful people blind to their deception.

"Our children need qualified teachers," they chant at jam-packed union rallies, yet the unions have created processes that require almost two school years to fire their incompetent members. They know that administrators can't speak about the egregious and nearly criminal behaviors of some of their least effective members, so they hide behind loopholes, technicalities, and half-truths. Meanwhile, we've got children graduating high schools reading at sixth-grade level, while others drop out and are shot dead in the streets.

When I met David Suker, I asked him what he'd done all day in the rubber room. "Played cards," he said. Apparently, spades was especially popular there. When I asked if he felt guilty about continuing to draw his $80,000 salary when he wasn't teaching, he said absolutely not. He said the system was flawed and that he was being unfairly punished.

I pointed out to Suker that, in his absence, there were still classes of kids who needed to be taught and therefore the district was getting double-dinged, paying for both him and his replacement. I pointed out that his $80,000 salary could pay for a season of varsity football for forty kids and their coaches, with enough money left over for varsity soccer, cross-country, cheerleading, and field hockey teams. I asked again if he felt guilty. "No," he said. He felt that *his* rights had been violated and the fact that he was being paid to play cards, as he'd done for hours the day we met, was the least that the district could do. Suker is also a single father.

The problem here is that *we* are the system: good people who believe in education are willing to have their taxes increased to pay for good schools—even if they send their own kids to private schools. We, not some make-believe boogieman or robber baron, are the ones shelling out $130 million per year in cities like New York for ineffectual teachers to hang out—doing nothing productive—all day every day in a rubber room or, as is the case in smaller districts, in the central office.

Chancellor Klein proposed a strategy to the teachers' union that would end the Dance of the Lemons. He requested that teachers who have been removed from the classroom be given six months' full salary and benefits while they look for another job. If they don't find one after almost a full school year, then the salary and benefits would end. The union refused.

If you consider the scenario I presented David Suker, you can begin to see how costly the union's practices are. Klein's $130 million spent on New York teachers placed in nonteaching reassignment centers just accounts for salaries and benefits; it doesn't include the cost of replacement teachers, which might potentially run another $130 million. It doesn't account for the estimated $200,000 it could cost to investigate and process each case. In 2010, there were approximately 550 teachers in rubber rooms. Some have been going to a nondescript building and sitting idle for thirteen years, but this is just the cost in money. Imagine how much music and art, after-school tutoring, summer and enrichment programs, sports, and amazing technology our children will never experience in public schools because we're paying so much to fire people who haven't been effective teachers.

Near the end of our CNN interview, I asked Suker if he was a good teacher. He told me he was the best that I'd ever see. Then he said, "Hire me." I told him that wasn't going to happen; however, I proposed, "If you're so good, why not get another job?" He said he'd put too much time into the district and was not going to walk away.

Thankfully, the rubber rooms have been closed in New York. Yet the problem persists. Today thousands of teachers who were removed from the classroom are still being paid not to teach all over the nation.

I THOUGHT MY battles with the local Hartford union were tough—and then I met Michelle Rhee, former chancellor of public schools in Washington, D.C. The teachers' union spent $1 million in the 2010 mayoral election to unseat the mayor who'd appointed her, thereby ensuring that she'd be removed. The union won. Mayor Adrian Fenty was defeated, but not before Rhee exposed the union to the nation. What's most revelatory is how she has inspired thousands of educators and made the first major gains in Washington's schools in nearly a generation.

Washington's schools were among the worst in the United States. They were dropout factories, places where teachers would take the paycheck and accept the status quo of failure. Every reform Rhee sought, the teachers' union fought.

The former chancellor did not back down. She fired over one thousand employees of the district and closed nearly thirty schools. "Reformers are trying to appeal to politicians' sense of good and right," she said, "but the unions are backing politicians who enable their dysfunction." She concluded by saying that "we are fighting the wrong fight and [the unions] are kicking our butts."

Here I disagree with Michelle Rhee. Good will always win. Fighting for kids will always be better than fighting for adults.

Look behind the curtain. Teachers' unions are the prime culprits responsible for bankrupting American public education. Union leaders spin their caring members into a swirl of emotion-driven obedience. They distort the truth and undermine progress so that they can keep getting that union check.

Michelle Rhee is just the most recent in a long line of educational reformers who fight for kids, which means fighting against education unions. The leaders of teachers' unions are the most powerful members of the education structure. They're a shadow regime controlling the fate of children, families, communities, and this nation. The dues of NEA and AFT's close to five million members make teachers' unions the biggest contributors to political campaigns of all interest groups.

If teachers' unions wanted to remove ineffective teachers from the classroom, ineffective teachers would disappear tomorrow. If teachers' unions wanted regressive politicians out of office, they'd be voted out of office. If teachers' unions wanted the achievement gap to disappear, they'd submit to accountability for all teachers.

Education unions, led by teachers' unions, are gatekeepers of the status quo. The unions' absolute commitment to *their* members' working conditions have failed to create a world-class public school system. They are in the way, and I want our children's futures back.

I have a direct challenge for the union leadership. The stakes couldn't be higher. We can divide the community in half: 50 percent union and 50 percent nonunion schools. Then let's compete. Winner takes all. Your schools will be run by your rules and ours will be run by ours. Your schools will operate under your own teacher, administrator, custodian, secretary, and security contracts. We'll settle on what works for us. And since you're always complaining that successful charter and magnet schools *cream*—that is, handpick—the best student applicants, we'll let you choose any kids you want, but we get to select all the *teachers* we want. After one academic year, we'll compare the two working models. Whoever ends with the most college applications and the best student results will win the contract for that city. Deal?

Evaluation Frustration

I UNDERSTAND WHY many education reformers have issues with tenure and the evaluation process for teachers. The complicated and onerous process of removing a teacher from the classroom is often discussed. It's rarely explained. The more you parents understand about how teachers are evaluated, the more concerned you'll become.

Even if a principal can prove that kids are not learning, he cannot use this as cause to fire a teacher. In fact—shocking as this may sound—principals are also not allowed to fire a teacher who has committed a crime unless this crime was committed while they were teaching . . . and it can be proved.

So, you may ask, what in the world *can* a teacher be fired for?

The answer is: very little. You begin to understand why so few teachers are ever fired.

All teachers, and in fact most public employees, have a right to due process. In the education sphere, this is a quasi-legal series of evaluations and consultations that a supervisor must employ before removing a teacher from a school.

Here is a real, and very typical, teacher evaluation process:

ACTIVITY	DUE DATE	WHAT SHOULD HAPPEN	WHAT DOES HAPPEN
Objective form: Teacher is asked to fill out objective form. These objectives reflect what the *teacher* thinks she could do to improve her teaching. Though the principal has to sign off, if the teacher does not agree with the principal's objectives, she does not have to sign the form.	Before mid-October	This form should state what students will know and be able to do. The principal should align all teaching and learning with best practices and students' learning needs. However, nothing that measures student performance can be included in this or any part of the process.	Teacher tells principal what she'd like to accomplish by the end of the year. This could be to have better classroom management or more organized lesson plans or to simply work better with colleagues.
Pre-observation conference and form: Teacher explains to principal what she will teach and what she'd like him to observe.	Prior to the principal's observation and before December	The principal and teacher should identify skills that students must know, along with proof that the kids have learned it during their lessons.	The principal and teacher agree on a class, date, and time that the principal will observe. The teacher will typically select the class and what she wants the principal to observe. *This point is very important because the teacher can only be evaluated on what is agreed upon.*

Formal observation and form: Two in a year. These are announced planned visits to the class to observe agreed-upon teaching strategies.	Before mid-December	The principal should come in unannounced to acquire proof that the teacher is teaching according to standards that meet or exceed those set by the state.	The teacher knows about and has had as much as two weeks to prepare for the observation.
Post-observation form: Principal discusses with the teacher his observations regarding what she did to meet the lesson's stated teaching goals.	Before December 15	Using student achievement data, teacher and principal discuss the teacher's effectiveness at delivering the observed lesson. Teacher offers proof to confirm or refute the principal's observations.	Based on the stated teaching goals, the principal determines if the teacher has done what she said she was going to do during that lesson. The teacher then replies either by refuting or by signing the form.

The teacher evaluation process in my district requires that I judge a growth plan (action research) created by a tenured teacher. This judgment has nothing to do with evaluating whether or not the teacher is effective; the assumption built into the evaluation instrument is that if you have tenure, you're effective. If I find a teacher to be ineffective, I have to provide him with support. It's at this point that I'm required to observe lessons and give feedback based on what I've observed in these planned visits. Yes, I can observe unannounced, but the formal process relies on planned visits where the teacher knows that I'm coming.

The principal is observing to confirm that the teacher is using the teaching strategies that he said he was going to use in the specific class that he wanted the principal to observe, on the day and at the time that they agreed on. In other words, the teacher under scrutiny *knows* when the principal is coming; he tells the principal what he wants him to look at.

And yet there's more. In the event that the two observations go badly, in many instances, a principal has to meet with the teacher and the school's union rep to explain why he feels the way he does! I'm the damn principal. Why would I—or anybody's boss—have to justify why, after multiple meetings and notifications, I'm not pleased with what I saw?

This is due process and so it's the *principal's* responsibility to outline exactly what he didn't like and then provide the teacher forty-five days to correct it by creating and implementing an intensive plan with support from the district. This requirement means that the principal has to assign the failing teacher a mentor in the building, send the teacher to a conference, or provide her with professional development so that she can be provided with additional opportunities to screw up your child's life.

Yes, while your child's principal is observing and filling out a total of fourteen different forms, not including additional documentation—the formal *justification* for his assessment of the teacher—your child is not learning, and there is not a damn thing you or your principal can do about it.

While your son's principal spends hours looking for a conference for this low-performing teacher to attend on classroom management, your son's advanced placement (AP) chemistry class is in a state of mayhem and, no, the college that you want him to attend is *not* going to accept "due process" or any other goofy-ass reason given for his not learning chemistry. The AP exam won't accept any excuses either.

Forty-five days after February brings us to mid-April. Therefore, your son's ineffective AP chemistry teacher, the same one you've called his entire junior year to complain about, the same one your principal has spent the last seven months documenting and supporting, gets yet *another* reprieve. The way it works here in Hartford, I have to give this teacher another forty-five days in which I must tell him exactly what I want him to do.

At the end of the second forty-five-day cycle, the principal can recommend that the teacher be terminated. Then the district has to pay the teacher while the termination hearing plays out. This can last months and costs thousands of dollars. Meanwhile, your son's AP chemistry class has a substitute teacher for the all-important junior year.

The hearing process is grueling. Who gets the focus of the abuse? The principal! He is cross-examined and questioned about every decision he made and every notation. Any failure to document or to communicate in writing renders the principal without a voice, with his credibility questioned. He has to leave the building to attend these hearings and may have to involve students, parents, or other staff members in this ugly hearing. The best-case scenario is that it'll take *only* two full years—your son's junior and senior years—and lots of money to get rid of a bad tenured teacher. Try explaining this to the college admissions rep when your son doesn't pass the AP chemistry or physics exams because he had a combination of horrible teachers and subs in his last two years of high school science. Good luck getting your son to ace organic chemistry and fulfill his dream of being a doctor.

Often the district will offer a deal. Yup, that's the education equivalent of a plea bargain. The deal generally includes paid leave time that counts toward retirement and even a letter of recommendation so that another district can be fooled into taking this teacher.

All staff, including but not limited to teachers, social workers, guidance counselors, vice principals, security guards, secretaries, custodians, and, yes, even the lunch ladies, have some form of the above-listed *due process*. A typical staff, which includes all of those previously mentioned, exists in a ratio of at least 50 to 1—staff members to administrator. The length of due process and the sheer number of staff in a school ensure that over 95 percent of all teachers in the United States will be back in the classrooms next year.

Due process is a legal designation that is available to nearly all public school employees, even when there are no unions in the schools. So the *removal of collective bargaining* in states like

Wisconsin *does not remove* due process; it just diminishes the impact of the union—a privately run organizationn—on the public's ability to provide essential and basic services.

At its best, due process is supposed to protect employees from discriminatory or capricious actions of supervisors. At its worst, it becomes a process that is so convoluted and burdensome that it severely limits, if not virtually eradicates, a principal's ability to remove bad teachers from the classroom in enough time to provide the students with a chance to catch up on what they missed while the failed teacher was in charge.

Teachers are virtually impossible to fire because the process that has been designed and supported by boards of education throughout the nation protects perfectly mediocre teachers. Short of something egregious or illegal occurring on the job, mediocre teachers are set for life.

If a teacher comes to work on time, has a decent rapport with the kids, hands in lesson plans, and goes to staff meetings, then he or she basically can't be let go. Showing up to practice and the games doesn't get you into the Hall of Fame, but just showing up at school will yield a thirty-seven-year career with retirement at 75 percent of the highest salary and health benefits for both the teacher and his or her spouse for the rest of their lives. *S-w-e-e-et!*

Where I differ from this process is that I let folks know that I'm not playing with them. You come to work at Capital Prep, you better come to *work*. We are watching every detail. Yes, we have read the contract; we know what it says and what is just *lore*.

Lore in this sense refers to what most public school employees *think* the contract says. For instance, most people I encounter believe that the principal can't come into the classroom without notifying the teacher first. Most teachers and administrators adhere to this belief and therefore teachers receive visits from only the administrators that have been pre-announced. The depth of this belief has created, for certain teachers, a myth of isolation and invincibility.

As I've said, I've dug into the contract and I've discovered that—surprise—I don't have to tell a questionable teacher jack. I can come and go as I please. Once I realized this, the entire power balance shifted in my school. The situation went from my thinking that I had to ask the teachers for *permission* to evaluate them to the way things are currently. At Capital Prep we have open-door classrooms in which parents, colleagues, and I feel comfortable visiting classrooms whenever we want.

I'm confident that most principals and teachers don't actually read the contracts. I keep copies of all of the union contracts on my desk at all times; this includes the union boilerplate for the custodians, security staff, lunch ladies, principals, and teachers. Principals who want to create an optimum school environment *must* read the contracts. This simple act of reading can shift the direction of a school.

For me, the happy result is that, so far, I have remained unbeaten by any union on any issue. Every teacher I removed is still gone. Every reform I've made remains intact. Even after multiple grievances and direct assaults on my character by the teachers' union—and after having had to deal with a picket line set up outside my school—the unions have had no real impact on Capital Prep beyond a buzzing annoyance. Admittedly, I can take this hard-line attitude because my staff is small.

Life-and-Death Stakes
of Accountability

AT THE START of the 2010–2011 academic year, a California teacher leapt off a bridge to his death. California teachers' union official Mathew Taylor later said he believed that the teacher's "less effective" ranking on a *Los Angeles Times* website was a contributing factor to the suicide. We'll probably never know why the thirty-nine-year-old fifth-grade teacher took his life. What's clear is that the high stakes of school accountability are growing steadily higher—often with tragic results.

Rigoberto Ruelas Jr. was found at the foot of a remote forest bridge. Ruelas scored "average" in getting his students up to acceptable levels in English, but "less effective" in math, and "less effective" overall. The middle school where he worked received an overall ranking of "least effective." Though thirty of the school's thirty-five teachers were ranked as less effective, Ruelas is the only teacher to have taken his life allegedly as a result of the *LA Times* publishing the scores.

The politicization of Ruelas's death shows how far both sides are willing to go in the argument over the process of determining what makes a good teacher. The tragedy of Ruelas's death cannot be overlooked nor can it be seen beyond the context of a man whose gifts could not save him from the challenges that eventually overtook him. The conversation that it has sparked marks a shift toward an increased expectation that teachers will be accountable individually for their impact on children.

Communities have developed quite an appetite for teacher accountability. When, in the summer of 2010, the *LA Times* began listing individual teacher rankings on its website, parents, politicians, and education reformers took notice. The reaction from both advocates of accountability and the teachers' unions—the most vocal detractors—was swift.

Our communities want more information on our schools' performance. Parents, you have become more sophisticated. You know that teachers make a difference in a child's academic life and now you want to use the available data so you can do more than select the right school. You want to put your child in front of the best teachers.

Something happened in 2010 that shifted Americans' focus to education. When the national economy collapsed in 2008, its impact wasn't really felt by public school systems until 2009–2010. As millions of home loans foreclosed, billions in property tax revenue dried up. Property taxes are the primary source of our local school budgets. Budget cuts lead quickly to layoffs in schools. And while this was happening, Americans were catching wind of our students' abysmal performance in international rankings of developed nations, even as our most successful domestic schools became harder to afford or attend. Almost overnight, people wanted simple answers: if the U.S. is spending so much money on education, why are our kids failing?

The domestic achievement gap would be better titled a *teaching* gap. As far back as 1998, we learned that the achievement gap that exists between African American, Latino, White, and Asian children as well as between poor and wealthy children could be eliminated if we could assign the best teachers to the worst schools. According to education theorist Andrew J. Wayne, the poorest American kids, regardless of race, are taught by teachers "who graduate from institutions rated either 'minimally difficult' or 'noncompetitive' " and those children are "21 percent and 39 percent in low- and high-poverty schools, respectively." According to Wayne, 60 percent of urban educators come from the lowest-ranked colleges in the country. Also, high school teachers in "schools serving disadvantaged populations are often less experienced and less knowledgeable about the subjects they teach than teachers in more affluent communities."*

The fact is, if you're in college and you're not terribly good at school, there's a good chance you'll become a public school teacher. If you are among the lowest performers, you could teach in one of the inner city's "dropout factories," and, as I stressed earlier, after just three short years you'll be tenured. This means that by the age of twenty-four you'll likely have a 95 percent chance of keeping that job for the rest of your working life.

Perhaps not surprisingly, given the grim working conditions, educators assigned to urban schools are absent from work far more often than suburban and rural educators. A University of California research study showed that schools with high levels of

....

*Wayne, Andrew J., http://epaa.asu.edu/ojs/article/view/309

minority and impoverished students are more likely to have substitute teachers than schools with suburban students. This study found that, at the most important psychological and academically crucial time in a child's life, the neediest students are receiving less—and a lower quality of—instruction.*

It's a simple fact: substitutes don't teach. When we have substitutes at Capital Prep, I'm very unhappy because no matter how good the lesson plans left behind, the kids end up essentially with a day off. A good sub hands out materials, turns on the movie, and keeps the kids from making too much noise. Substitute teachers are doing little more than babysitting students who need the most qualified teachers.

How in the hell are we going to get America's students caught up to the rest of the developed world when our teachers are missing so many days? Coming to work is about professionalism and respect for the children. Teachers who feel that it is their *right* to take all the days that they're allotted should exercise their right to do something else for a living. Otherwise, get your lazy asses out of bed and go teach our kids.

Research from Tennessee, a state where teachers' ability is measured and quantified, found that the lowest-performing teachers produced minimal gains of 15 points on standardized exams. The most skilled teachers produced gains of 53 points during this same time on the same exams.**

Effective teachers matter. This same study stated that an ef-

---

*Bruno, James E., http://epaa.asu.edu/epaa/v10n32
**Haycock, K., http://academic.research.microsoft.com/Author/587085/k=haycock

fective teacher could move her students as much as a year and a half ahead of a mediocre teacher's students during the same time.

Education theorists like Wayne and Haycock posit that smarter teachers produce smarter students. Of course, smart teachers who *inspire* kids matter most of all, but at the end of the day, it's enough that the teacher is simply smarter. The rationale is that smarter teachers have more information to give students and that this fuels student learning.

Why might students learn more from teachers with better academic skills? Teachers who read faster may acquire new content knowledge more quickly. Teachers with greater verbal facility may spend their preparation time more focused on lesson design than on deciding what exactly to say. Maybe teachers with better college entrance examination scores learned more in college, or maybe entrance examination scores and college selectivity correlate with the quality of teachers' pre-collegiate education—a much longer educational experience than undergraduate education.

This latest academic research by theorists like Wayne and Haycock is supported by the things I see each day as a principal. Elite private college-preparatory schools are most often staffed by alums of elite private college-preparatory schools and/or elite liberal arts colleges. Thus smart people from good schools teach at the best schools and their students excel. Imagine that.

Public schools require that teachers be certified. Even though there is no evidence that certification improves instruction, legislators and teachers' unions keep this practice in place. The problem is that many of the nation's most prestigious colleges are liberal arts focused and do not offer teacher certification programs. Even if they did, to teach in a public school, prospective teachers would still need certification in the state within which they wanted to teach. Worse, smart people wishing to change careers meet the roadblock of certification, which often requires them to go back to an education school to "learn to teach."

Think about what this means in practice. If an internationally renowned brain surgeon wants to teach biology in a public school, she cannot. Astronauts can't teach physics, nor can professional athletes teach gym. Donald Trump can't teach basic math in a Harlem public school; Warren Buffett can't teach a business class; and Bill Gates, a man who has funded hundreds of successful schools and educated thousands of disadvantaged children the world over, cannot teach in a Seattle public school. Neither Barack nor Michelle Obama can teach civics in a Washington, D.C., public school. Of course, all these notable Americans could teach in our most elite private colleges, universities, and high schools. None can be hired by a needy public school.

Education reformers have sought to create methods of informing and ensuring parents that their children are being taught by the most skilled people. While chancellor of the D.C. public school system, Michelle Rhee sought to institute a novel evaluation system that combined accountability and rewards, including a pay-for-performance system that would have compensated the highest-performing teachers to upward of $140,000. Not surprisingly, the D.C. teachers' union fought this proposal because it gave too much power to the principal to determine who is or isn't a good teacher.

As was widely reported in the national media, and vividly depicted in *Waiting for Superman,* the Washington Teachers' Union felt that employing data such as student performance on the district's standardized test scores to assess teacher effectiveness was unfair to teachers. The union cited the limitations that race and class have on student achievement. As we've seen, while race does matter, it only matters in that it impacts who is teaching the children. Race and class have no impact on how much a child can learn. The union's stance is, in fact, both wrong and implicitly racist.

I agree with one of the union's contentions: that test scores *alone* do not a good teacher make. I also agree with the union's assertion that too few principals are aware of what a good teacher is; therefore, too few can be trusted to determine if the teacher is effective. Where we part ways is in our reaction to what needs to be done. I believe that we should use standardized measures, including but not limited to students' performance on tests, student evaluations of teachers, and attendance and graduation rates, as well as other observable yet not currently standardized characteristics such as hours teachers spend leading extracurricular activities and their ability to build meaningful relationships.

While reasonable people can disagree about the details of methodology, there's no disputing that Michelle Rhee and former chancellor of New York City's public schools Joel Klein have put viable solutions on the table. They've developed comprehensive and elaborate evaluation plans that could—if we show the political backbone—ensure that only the most effective teachers are allowed in the classroom.

PART SIX

Outdated

Strap Up

I'M OFTEN SURPRISED that groups invite me to speak. Yusuf Salaam is my longtime publicist—or as I often tell him, he's the man with the hardest job on earth. People catch me on TV, blasting off on a group—teachers' unions, professional agitators, know-it-all pundits—about which they feel similarly. Then they holler at Yusuf and book me.

College kids are great: they just want me to fly off the handle. For them, I can't go hard enough, be irreverent enough or bold enough. The more I challenge the status quo, the more they want to hear it. Doesn't matter what the audience makeup is—Black, White, Hispanic, Asian—the kids demand the raw, uncut truth.

On the other hand, we get requests from groups who think they're booking the education version of Barack Obama: a polite, conciliatory Black guy who is going to make them comfortable. Well, that's when things get interesting.

Yusuf dutifully tells me, "They want an idea of what you're going to say."

He knows damn well what my response is, but he's stuck.

"Tell them to be there when I say it and we'll both find out at the same time."

I am *out* of patience. I work in schools, but not in academia. Academics study trends and statistics. I'm trying to end trends and stop my kids from becoming statistics. When I meet these lifelong liberals, I nod and smile and tell myself, *They're nice enough people.* When they got started in their careers, I was getting started in life. Hell, I wasn't even born when many of them made a name for themselves. I respect them, the way I respect great-aunts and uncles who've told that story too many times.

Save it for the reunion—I've gotta get kids to graduation.

Of, for, and by the People

CUT THAT GRAY ponytail; turn off the Peter, Paul and Mary records; put away that tie-dyed T-shirt; and cancel every commemorative march planned for Dr. King's birthday. Here's the truth, folks: hippies, academics, and civil rights relics *are* the system that they claim to detest.

Parents, you know you're being jerked around; you just don't know who's doing it or how. Somebody has to be accountable for the failures in public education and everybody can't keep blaming parents. You've accepted your responsibility. You know you've worked too much, struggled with your own issues, and stumbled through your relationships. But even if you accepted all of the blame you possibly could, there would still be an international achievement gap.

I've got news for you. Politics is just that—freakin' politics. Toggle back and forth between the shouting talking heads on CNN, MSNBC, and Fox News. At best, our current political system is a high-stakes game of one-upmanship. At worst, it's a glorified, brightly lit theater of hypocrisy. Politics is not designed to solve problems. In fact, its primary purpose is to maintain long-held divisions. Our kids' schools need to improve *now* and we have to look beyond the traditional lines of left and right, liberals and conservatives, and dive headlong into the facts. Yes, the *facts*. Even if an American student attends a good school in a good neighborhood, the odds are that she'll still be one of the lowest-performing students in the industrialized world.

The truth stings our pride, I know. But we have to ask: how did we get to this pathetic state? Simply put, we got here because we were wrong. Americans believed that race mattered when it came to group and individual performance. White folks moved to White suburbs. Black people sought integrated schools while judges, politicians, civil rights relics, and hippies recited stanzas from Martin Luther King's "I Have a Dream" speech and America's schoolchildren fell behind.

In 1954, no doubt, the civil rights workers were in the vanguard. And they were right on the issues. Brown needed to defeat the Board of Education in Topeka, Kansas. Segregation was the closet in which America's ugliest skeletons could be found. In 1964, they were right. America needed to pass the Civil Rights Act so the basic human rights of women and minorities could be recognized and later protected. Government programs were the perceived answer and enlisting in the War on Poverty was essential. The laws and social programs that came from these times remain examples of the very best humanity has to offer those who are disenfranchised by their government as a result of unearned disadvantages.

But here's the problem: today's issues are more nuanced and complex. Relying on those same strategies—no matter how effective and right they were in the 1960s—is like sending an infantryman into Afghanistan armed with a musket.

Hippies, academics, and civil rights relics have spent the last two generations focusing on "The System"—the amorphous

System—that convoluted set of socioeconomic factors, re-sources, and permanent conditions such as race and poverty. For sixty years, they've told us that if we can just end racism and poverty, then we will have equality in all forms. To achieve this end, they've tried it all. They took over college buildings as kids, served in the Peace Corps as young adults, and then became part of the very System they vowed to change. The results? Persistent and deeper poverty, ever-declining student performance, and the emergence of an even deeper international achievement gap.

Enough with the poverty and race argument. Enough with be-lieving that wealth and Whiteness will lead to academic success.

These hippies, academics, and civil rights relics are wrong. Nice, sweet, old, and wrong. They are so wrong that it feels like we're in a 2011 living room, huddled around a fuzzy black-and-white waiting for Elvis to come on the *Ed Sullivan Show* while the rest of the world leans back to take in Lady Gaga on a 120-inch HD 3D flat-screen.

Closing of the Old School

JONATHAN KOZOL IS among the most respected academics writing and speaking on public education. His work spans generations. He kicked off his career in education back in 1960, as a teacher in the Boston Public Schools system, where he was reportedly fired for teaching a Langston Hughes poem. Since then, he's spoken throughout the world about the inequities in American public education. For fifty years and in some twelve nonfiction books—most notably *Savage Inequalities: Children in America's Schools*—he has railed against racism, classism, and conservatism. In his work, he always returns to his essential question: "Is it right that the place of one's birth should determine the quality of one's education?"

Kozol has made a career writing and talking about these disparities. Over and over, he argues that poor districts receive less money than wealthy districts. This disparity seems logical, right? Tax dollars make up school budgets. Poorer districts, with far more renters than tax-paying property owners, kick in far less money.

There's one problem with Kozol's premise. It's dead wrong. Hartford, Connecticut—where I live and work—is the second-poorest city per capita in the United States of America. Our per capita income here is just over $13,000. Greenwich, Connecticut, just seventy-one miles away, is one of the wealthiest cities in America. Some of the *world's* wealthiest people live in Greenwich. Yet both Hartford and Greenwich spend $14,000 per student. In fact, Hartford has spent almost half a billion—yes, *billion*—on school construction in the past five years. Hartford remains in the 95th percentile in overall performance, while Greenwich is in the 5th percentile.

Not long ago, I interviewed Cory Booker, mayor of Newark, New Jersey. Mayor Booker told me that his very poor city— again, among the most impoverished in the nation—spends $22,000 per student per year. Staggering. That's more than 90 percent of all school districts in America spend! Yet for several generations now, Newark has failed to educate its children who attend public schools.

I can hear your skepticism. Jonathan Kozol is *wrong* on education policy? Who could question a Harvard-educated Rhodes Scholar—holder of two Guggenheim fellowships and winner of the National Book Award—a man who left Cambridge to study in Paris, only to return to deeply segregated Roxbury, Massachusetts, to tutor disadvantaged Black kids?

Me. The truth is the truth. Yes, Jonathan Kozol is wrong. Kozol rails against vouchers because he sees them as a code word for resegregation. But the forced segregation of 1954 is not the same as giving parents educational options in 2011. Today, many "schools of choice"—particularly high-performing inner-city ones—have greater resources than public schools in suburban districts. They've got better science and computer labs, performance spaces, more languages being taught, and higher college-going rates than even the good suburban schools. Sure, these schools are located in the 'hood, but they're newer and a lot more impressive than some "Whiter" and wealthier schools. It's not the same discussion. It's not *Plessy v. Ferguson*. This is about good schools that are open to all kids but are most often utilized by students of color.

For millions of American children who are trapped by geography—stuck living in failing, dysfunctional districts—school choice offers the only hope of getting access to quality education. So-called education reformers like Kozol require that parents be patient, to wait five more years for school reform to *possibly* take hold. Even though none of these proposed reforms have worked in the last fifty years, he's still advocating them.

I'm not an academic; I'm a practitioner. I don't have the time to pore over statistics; I have to stop kids from becoming statistics. I want your kids to go to good schools now. Absolute choice, including public money being spent in private schools (voucher), must be open to all students, rich or poor, Black, White, and other.

Why challenge a sweet, grandfatherly man who's spent his life writing and talking about public education? Because I have zero interest in esoteric academic babblings that after a half century have yet to actually take shape. I currently exist on the frontlines. I need to deliver now. I need to be able to look every kid in the face, point, and say, like Oprah giving away cars, "Now *you* get a good school and *you* get a good school and *you* get a good school!"

I once saw Jonathan Kozol speak at St. Joseph's College in Connecticut and, *damn,* wasn't he *adorable* the way he broke into baby talk as he described the brilliant but underperforming middle-school girl whom he'd met in a failed school. I could almost feel him patronizingly patting me on the head as he felt *our* pain. His own kids and grandkids will never set foot in a failed school for any other purpose than to research it. Yet he's so committed to fighting for our kids by ensuring that they will never have a choice to attend a successful school outside their neighborhood.

Kozol behaves like an anthropologist—however empathetic—deigning to live among the savages and spread his doctrine of savage inequalities. Wouldn't it be nice to be granted a platform from which to pontificate for the past fifty years?

Here's the question I have for Mr. Kozol and his ilk. During those past fifty years, have you *solved* one damn problem? You have called yourself an education reformer, yet tell me which schools, in which part of the country, are producing better-educated students because of your long-discussed theories? Which failed schools have you shut down? Which teachers, principals, and administrators have you removed? In our poorest communities, our schools are in the sorriest state ever, and the scourge of low expectations that you've injected into the debate has made its way into the 'burbs now.

DIANE RAVITCH IS Kozol's female alter ego—a supposed education "guru" and best-selling author in her own right. Ravitch made her name in the highest levels of government during the administrations of George H. W. Bush and Bill Clinton. She is now a professor at New York University's Steinhardt School of Culture, Education, and Human Development. In her writings, Ravitch appears pained by the notion that schools could close—or worse, be privatized or chartered.

In her work, like last year's *The Death and Life of the Great American School System: How Testing and Choice Are Undermining Education,* Ravitch claims—rightly—that the No Child Left Behind Act of 2001 shows little hope of improving America's antiquated and poorly performing neighborhood schools. But so what? The legislation is called No *Child* Left Behind—NCLB. It's not called No *School* Left Behind or No *Teacher* Left Behind or No *Principal* Left Behind. The law is quite willing to leave behind failed schools and disperse the students to better schools.

Let's talk about NCLB. Congressmen and a former president grew sick and tired of paying billions in salaries to public school employees so that they could keep their jobs and pensions. Yes, push has come to shove and the federal government finally got fed up. In a bipartisan effort, they said enough is a damn 'nuff. If taxpayers—the "we" in "we, the people"—are going to provide the local districts with billions of dollars to educate America's children, then *we* expect them to be able to read, write, and compute on grade level. (How sad has the state of public education become that the promise of schools teaching all children to read, write, and compute on grade level is a revolutionary concept?)

When bad schools close, we all win. The community gets to spend the money on programs and schools that work. The kids gain access to schools that teach. Even the staff and faculty have the opportunity to work for a winning team.

Side note: All of the staff we hired in the first few years at Capital Prep came from failed schools. Not a *single* one came from a successful school. But when they were put in a better system, better things happened. There are no losers when dysfunctional schools close. None.

Ravitch's primary issue is with privatization. She and her cohort would have you believe that any effort to create or support private education with public money is inherently evil. They predict mass destruction if public money, currently tied to failing neighborhood schools, were to "follow the child" to a more effective charter, magnet, or private school.

What I find hypocritical is that almost all her supporters are fellow professors at the most expensive elite private colleges and parents who live exclusively in swanky suburbs.

How in the hell do you argue against privatization from a privately funded professor's position at an elite private university? Are you serious? Who else can the antiprivatization argument be made to except other professors at other elite private universities? Who else will support this blatant hypocrisy? Oh, let me guess—all the teachers and union leaders who share billions of dollars and a lifetime guarantee of uninterrupted employment as long as the current oligarchy of neighborhood public education is maintained?

How does Ravitch justify public money—federal student financial aid—being spent for education at the fine private institutions where she has taught, Columbia University and New York University? Federal student financial aid is an education *voucher* that no one would argue has brought harm to education or access to education. In fact, most would say the opposite: that if it were not for federally subsidized student loans and grants, many students would never have been able to attend or graduate from college. I know I wouldn't have gotten through college without financial aid. Good looking out, Senator Pell.

Ravitch contends that her viewpoint was shaped in the middle of the last century. In today's fast-changing educational landscape, it may as well have been four hundred years ago. Back when she was a kid in mid-1940s Houston, Texas, Ravitch says she was denied access to a private school because she's Jewish. (She still managed to get into Wellesley College and Columbia University.) In those days, of course, private schools, universities, and country clubs were largely "restricted"—Jews, Asians, and Blacks had little hope of gaining entry. This apparently profoundly shaped Ravitch's identity. She's written that this experience in the 1940s made her and her family staunch supporters of neighborhood public schools. As a child of the segregated South, she became deeply suspicious of school choice.

Yet even as Ravitch fights for federal academic standards, she rails against standardized tests and federal policies like NCLB that seek to redress the results of *not* having national standards. The stated purpose of the NCLB legislation is to make sure that every child is educated to the same level. Isn't that what she wants? Isn't that precisely why she claims to support integration? So what's her beef with NCLB? Ravitch claims that it punishes schools that don't educate all kids equally. School integration ain't enough when the classrooms and expectations are not the same for all kids. Can NCLB be tweaked? Hell, yeah. It's a living piece of legislation, not the Bible. The real Diane Ravitch is against NCLB because the union is against the NCLB. She is a member of the Albert Shanker Institute, an organization named for the teachers' union's legendary president. She's also the recipient of the UFT's 2005 John Dewey Award.

A popular argument against NCLB is that it calls for "unfunded mandates." That means when a school fails for five years, the district has to offer kids remediation through tutoring, Saturday school, or, as a last resort, the option to attend another, better public school in the district—assuming there is one. Opponents claim that the government doesn't provide these failed schools with additional money to pay for the aforementioned mandated services—hence, the result is "unfunded mandates."

But the feds are really saying something pretty simple: *Hold up! We just paid you to educate. You did not deliver.* YOU MUST EDUCATE—*even if that means you have to pay somebody else to do it because you happen to be . . . well, incompetent!*

Parents, do you *really* care who receives the money for doing education right? Does it matter if the YMCA runs the after-school program? How would you feel if the school received funds from the United Way or the Gates Foundation? These are the mean-old *private* organizations that the clowns are actually fighting. Do you *really* want to keep paying taxes to have education done wrong? I don't know about you, but I've had it with the excuses. I just want results now. We pay good money for good schools and if George W. Bush's NCLB is going to provide all children access to them, then thank you very much, George W.

Privatization is not inherently bad. Bad schools are bad. A bad school is one that doesn't meet a family's needs, whether it be public or private. That same school could be perfect for another student. For many years, the problem with the school choice debate was that the legislators and academics making the decisions were too far removed from the children, too far from the solution—so they kept stepping on the problem.

I actually agree with Kozol's contention that a child's destiny should not be determined by her address. What I profoundly disagree with is how this should be dealt with. Kozol and Ravitch are committed to neighborhood schools. I'm committed to improving kids' chances of attending good schools—no matter where they are, no matter who runs them—as long as the kids can have access to them while they're still young.

Kozol and Ravitch are against any education option outside of their neighborhood. I'm for any education option that works *now*. These two education advocates are shaped by what used to be. I am compelled by what is. I live in the here and now. They live in some nostalgic past and a rosy future that has never materialized. When you have the luxury of working at our nation's best colleges and can brown-bag-lunch your way through discussions of race and class on the quad, it's easy to lose focus on what matters—good schools for all children right now.

Ravitch contends that "the best predictor of academic performance is poverty—not bad teachers." Two problems with this. First, she and all those who peddle this notion are wrong. The nation has hundreds of examples of very successful schools and thousands of classrooms filled with amazing teachers and their poor successful students. To accept this lie would be to discount a hundred years of successful educators in public and private schools. Second, if she is right, then we may as well shut down all schools with poor students in them, because they *ain't gonna learn no way*. . . .

The Intern and the Senator

WHEN I WAS IN college, I interned for United States senator Joseph I. Lieberman. Back when he was a Democrat. I'm not particularly proud of this. I was a kid and my mentors at the time told me that the internship would help me. They were right, but not in the way I'd anticipated. . . .

One day, I was manning the 800 line. This assignment meant that I had to respond to whoever called, and they could, and would, say anything. We spent hours listening to left-wing doves pissed off about Lieberman's decision to support the invasion of Iraq and fiscal hawks outraged that he'd voted himself a significant raise in a late-night session on the Hill.

When on the 800 line, we wouldn't talk back; we'd politely listen and tell the caller that we'd pass along the message to the senator. Of course, none of us spoke directly to Senator Lieberman. A little white lie, but we were all college kids who were working our asses off for no money, hoping for the prestige to kick in.

I'd just turned twenty years old and was majoring in political science and minoring in African American studies. My mom was the vice president in our public housing project. I'd worked for a mayor and canvassed for Jesse Jackson in his 1988 bid for president. I felt I came from a politically savvy background and had a good grasp of the civil rights movement—past and present. More important, I felt comfortable that what I'd learned was necessary to change public policy.

One night on the 800 line, I fielded a call from a mother in a New Haven housing project. She too was an officer in her tenant association. She didn't want much from Senator Lieberman. She simply wanted to get more police in one of the most dangerous neighborhoods. She'd marched in the past, she told me, and was ready to do it again. One of the senator's staffers told me to write up the lady's complaint and it would be addressed. I knew this meant she'd get a form letter signed by a machine that could replicate the senator's signature.

I wasn't very good on the 800 line. It was high-volume work, a meat grinder of sorts. I simply didn't process enough calls. My next assignment was the mailroom. I went from answering phones to being the guy assigned to discover if there was any mysterious white powder in an envelope.

Day after day, I'd sit in the mailroom, a dean's list student, buttoned up in my dress shirt and tie. One morning, a knot of letters—all from physicians—was delivered. A bunch of Connecticut doctors were simultaneously lobbying the senator to take their position on some medical issue. To me, it seemed like a convoy of dump trucks had arrived with nothing but these doctors' letters. It was my job to open every single one. The strange thing was that each letter was exactly the same. They were form letters, printed on various physicians' letterheads, simultaneously blitzing the senator. The office immediately went into panic mode. Every letter from a doctor's office had to be immediately answered!

The Office of Senator Joseph I. Lieberman—that was how we had to sign the letters—was twenty-one floors above the street, in an air-conditioned, highly secure building. If the lady from the New Haven housing projects, or my own mother from the Middletown projects, had taken five buses and spent all day in the hot July sun picketing, not one person in the senator's office would have noticed. On the other hand, with no fanfare, no mention on the evening news, these well-organized physicians had sent our office into a week-long frenzy.

That was it—lesson learned. Even as a young kid, I saw that you have to use new tactics if you want to change government. And I witnessed firsthand that politicians are cheap and easy to influence. Hippies, academics, and civil rights relics are like toy soldiers in a Labor Day parade. This old guard of the left consistently employs outdated and ineffective tactics. Yes, politicians will patronizingly applaud, maybe give them a little lip service at the press conference. In the meantime, they keep one eye on their humming BlackBerry that's delivering *real* marching orders from organized and surgically placed political lobbyists.

PART SEVEN

Solutions

Leaders of the New School

THE OPPORTUNITY—and urgent necessity—to fix our neighborhood schools has arrived in the unlikely guise of a major economic recession. This will demand both pride and innovation. It's time that educational entrepreneurs devise new models for education. Time for teachers to use the Internet to transport classrooms to China. Time to turn an RV into a classroom that travels from coast to coast teaching children the key laws of each state. That RV could become a convoy of young envoys traveling from state to state studying and impacting the local economy. Campers could plant themselves in Appalachia to study the peculiar relationships between race and class in these largely White mountain communities. Each marking period could offer the academic explorers new adventures and relevant research. The world is life's classroom, so why wait for graduation—why wait for the freedom of college—to go to school?

In my vision, math and science would come to life every day in these new schools. Social studies would really be a study of social institutions. English would be used for what it was intended, to communicate with people, not to showcase vocabulary words. Learning would be relevant and individualized. Skills would connect to the faces of the people our traveling students meet along their journey. Politics would have a face that is neither distant nor purely academic. Memorization would be replaced by learning. All these things and so much more would be extended to children. College and graduate school need not be the first time that ambitious students get the opportunity to leave the building to do something other than collect samples in a nearby field.

I believe that inspired educators *will* be found in corporate America. Savvy educators are ready for the rough waters of teaching children with low parental engagement, low skills, and low self-esteem. Here, in today's troubled economy, is where we learn that big old schools are not the answer, nor have they ever been for all kids. Here, in these resource-starved times, is where education can and must be reinvented. Small schools must cease to be the distinct luxury of the well-to-do. Vouchers will make that possible.

One teacher standing in front of a class of twenty-two children, all of whom must fight the urge to answer their buzzing BlackBerrys and iPhones, just won't cut it. As multimillion-dollar, unmanned aircraft whiz seven thousand miles from their pilots, teachers switch between red and black dry-erase markers in a vain effort to keep students' attention. In an age when children communicate in real time with the world, when the Sudan is a mouse click away, our kids are still sitting isolated for forty-five minutes, followed by three minutes to pass to another isolated classroom for forty-five minutes. As the world races to explore the new frontier of sustainable man-made energy, our kids' intelligence is being measured by standardized tests requiring regurgitation of facts and figures from outdated textbooks.

Technology is more than just a tool; it's a method for teaching. Amazing teachers are now available to all children with a click of the mouse. Children can learn math from a master, and all local districts can afford it. I can't hire a teacher to teach a few kids Arabic, but I can purchase a site license for a language program.

While gifted and talented programs lose their funding, universities like Johns Hopkins, Duke, and Stanford offer children as young as five the opportunity to take high-level courses at their own pace. Children with learning disabilities can now compensate for what nature has not given them through the use of programs that are designed to read to them, provide them with practice in math, or simply help them focus. As music programs are cut, students can learn to play an instrument with the assistance of technology.

The one-room schoolhouse of a hundred and fifty years ago grew into a massive high school where today's children feel lost and unloved. We know what they need and we can give it to them. Limited only by our *will* to change, we can and must build on what we know.

We must open our minds to the new school.

New Schools, Old Books

THE CORE ELEMENTS of today's public education system are the same as they were in the 1800s. Education is the only industry that has shown no fundamental change—which is amazing when you think about it. If the medical industry were still using nineteenth-century medicine, leaches and whiskey bottles would be stocked high in dirty clinics.

Nowhere is this disconnect more visible than in our "required reading" lists. The current design of public schools ensures that children will almost never read the most popular, engaging, diverse, and relevant books. As beautiful, thoughtful new political discourse is blogged every minute, our kids are weighed down with book bags bulging with George Orwell's *Animal Farm* (1945) and Charles Dickens's *Great Expectations* (1861). They're great novels, sure, but not exactly *fresh*.

The stacks of Barnes & Noble, Borders, Amazon, and thousands of independent booksellers—as well as the folding tables of African brothers on 125th Street in Harlem—are chock-full of books that kids will never have the time or the opportunity to read. Every week, publishers are releasing fantastic works of fiction and nonfiction, but our kids are forced to read thousands of pages of books that have no connection to their lives. Then we wonder, why don't our kids read?

The Internet bursts with writers, readers, and communities of people who love learning. It depicts an ever-changing world in which new ideas are formed and old ones cast aside. The Web, unlike TV, is a fully interactive medium in which even history is being rewritten—yet schools are still buying ten-pound text-books. Our kids know their way around the Net as well as they know the route to the bathroom. Obviously, a lot of Internet content isn't age-appropriate, but enough of it is for schools to fully integrate it into most every day.

Schools are not using current literature for a few reasons. The first, said politely, is comfort. These are often the books teachers read in high school and learned in college how to teach. To put it more bluntly, teachers cling to the old books because they're too lazy to write new lessons, learn new ways to teach old themes, or even ask the kids where they get their news and entertainment. Kids today are actually watching less and less TV because they're on the Internet. When are we educators going to get a clue? Kids want to read as much as *we* want to read.

A few years back, on a sunny winter day, I was in Harlem visiting an independent Black-owned bookstore called Sisters Uptown. While the adults got caught up in some deep political conversation, I noticed a Black girl who looked about twelve or thirteen. She was oblivious to the loud-talking adults. Huddled in a corner, she was reading one of the early Harry Potter books. I was stunned.

I slipped away from the adult conversation, wanting to know why this little Black girl was feverishly reading on a

Saturday evening. So I stood over her, draped her with my shadow, and asked her. She stopped reading long enough to tell me that she and her friends were competing to get to the end of the book.

"You must really like to read," I commented.

"Nope," she shot back, her thumbnail pinning back the hundreds of pages she'd already completed.

"So why are you reading this?"

And without even looking up at me, she said, "Because it's good."

The Harry Potter series is one of the world's true blockbusters, a bestseller second only to the Bible, yet it is not taught in most schools. Even if it were taught only to *criticize* it, the children would be reading—engrossed, using their imagination, expanding their vocabulary.

Schools are paralyzed by their fear of assigning offensive literature. If we've learned anything, it's that book burning ignites the fires of interest and the desire for many kids to even consider reading. Save the fire and ignite the interest in learning.

Anytime politics drives instruction, things go wrong. Great books are ripped from kids' hands; Darwin's theory of evolution through natural selection loses to the Immaculate Conception. Are some books classics? No doubt. But what exactly does that mean? Can't we teach about social injustice by using a book other than *To Kill a Mockingbird*? While Harper Lee, the Pulitzer Prize–winning author, would no doubt be flattered that we're still buying and teaching her novel, I'd be willing to bet that both Lee and William Golding, the Nobel laureate author of *Lord of the Flies*, would have envisioned that by 2011, there'd be new socially and politically edgy novels from which kids could learn essential concepts.

The adolescent isolation and angst of Holden Caulfield and Ponyboy Curtis no longer resonate with kids growing up in the age of social networking. Hell, I love Holden's wanderings through late-1940s Manhattan, but *come on!* Holden would be a great-grandfather today. Of course, I do believe that some of the classics should be taught, since they're part of our heritage. Therefore, at Capital Prep, our English department does teach them—but not exclusively. We refer to both the *New York Times* and *Essence* magazine for the skinny on hot books. We want our kids to be able to read a book that their parents are reading instead of one they can vaguely remember.

We're told repeatedly that the argument for continuing to read these traditional books is that our kids *need* to read them to be successful in college and in life. You bet they need to read them—*if* they're going to major in English or comp lit or plan on becoming a humanities professor. Shakespeare may be the greatest and most influential writer in the history of English literature, but most high school English teachers would be hard pressed to teach *Hamlet, Macbeth,* or *Romeo and Juliet* without having a Shakespeare study guide and an *Oxford English Dictionary* in their top desk drawer.

The themes of these plays are timeless and continue to resonate in youth culture. The wildly popular High School Musical series works straight off the *Romeo and Juliet* template. *The Lion King* is an obvious—and infectious—adaptation of *Hamlet.* For kids who are utterly mystified by the Elizabethan English and iambic pentameter—who can't tell a thane from a liege—would it be so wrong for teachers to assign a *High School Musical* novelization, or a *Lion King* DVD, as an entrée into the world and themes of Shakespeare?

Let's be honest, even without a deep understanding of Shakespeare, Melville, or Mark Twain, the rest of us will do just fine left with the billions of words on the Web and the books crowding today's bestseller lists. We often forget that few of the foreign students who come to the U.S. and succeed—vaulting past our homegrown kids—have read *The Grapes of Wrath* or *To Kill a Mockingbird,* let alone the comedies and tragedies of Shakespeare.

All kids who can read *do* read something. The challenge for educators is to figure out what they want to read and learn how to teach from that.

Take a minute: look in your kids' book bags. There you will find, amazingly, BOOKS! No, they're not all great—or even good—but they *are* books. Science fiction, erotica, and street crime novels, as well as the Twilight, 39 Clues, and Diary of a Wimpy Kid series, have turned many kids on to reading. Of course, we don't want them reading soft porn or too much profanity, but when they do, we can use it as a teachable moment. We can break down the distinction between pulpy sensationalism and higher-quality fiction. At Capital Prep, I've witnessed the most popular titles in our kids' book bags getting passed around like a well-worn 1980s *Playboy* magazine lifted from an older brother.

Technology is too great to be burdening kids with our out-dated books. The Kindle, Nook, and iPad may not yet have the capacity to replace the printed word, but that day is not far away. Unlike many adults, kids don't have a problem reading off a computer screen. In our classrooms, we are employing Smart Boards. Our teachers use them as tools to teach so many skills. It seems clear that we're just a few years from arriving at a time when textbooks are obsolete. Schools must learn to adapt or die.

Keep in mind, with the latest cell phones, there is more information at your fingertips than there is in a high school library. This has presented my staff at Capital Prep with a particular challenge. We began construction of our school in 2008. We were awarded the money in 2004. Our plans called for a library. We now have one, but to be frank, we aren't sure what we're going to do with it. We're in the process of going paperless. Our kids are just a few years away from carrying a library in their pockets. So during the worst recession of our lives, should we spend hundreds of thousands of dollars to order thousands of books and have them sit, immaculately stacked and unopened, or should we use that money to buy Kindles, Nooks, and other electronic readers? To date, our 10,000-square-foot library has only a small collection of books—donated by parents, teachers, and benefactors.

Schools must meet and then lead innovation. We've got to revamp both *what* we're teaching and *how*. New texts and new technology must go hand in hand; otherwise we lose both the children and our seat in the fast-changing, technologically advanced modern economy.

Selected List of Current Best-Selling and Notable Young Adult Books

1. The Hunger Games trilogy, by Suzanne Collins

2. *Keeping the Moon,* by Sarah Dessen

3. *Eragon,* by Christopher Paolini

4. *When You Reach Me,* by Rebecca Stead

5. *The 39 Clues: The Maze of Bones,* by Rick Riordan

Cracking the AP Myth

ONE STRATEGY WE'VE used effectively at Capital Prep is to enroll kids in college while still in high school. It's built into our design. We're an *early-college* high school. We didn't invent the concept: LaGuardia Community College in Queens, New York, was among the first in the country to offer high school students college classes back in the early 1970s.

Back then, the rationale was to demystify college for students not likely to go on to institutions of higher learning. LaGuardia opened its doors to the high school students—and guess what? They excelled. This program was designed to both remediate these at-risk kids and then to transition them into college. LaGuardia's early-college model has since spawned others throughout the country that serve primarily low-income students.

But to focus on who started the early-college program would be missing the greater point. Even the best kids struggle in advanced placement (AP) courses. Hell, AP courses are *meant* to be hard. They're like high school courses on steroids; their only contribution to kids' high school experience is more zits and stress. What's worse is that after the grueling process is over, if you don't get a 4 or 5 on the AP exam, you get no college credit. Indeed, if you earn anything less than a high B, it does nothing to improve your standing among college admissions reps. A frustrating situation all round, since most kids in AP are doing it to enter the big leagues, or better yet, the Ivy League.

Everyone can learn from strategies originally developed for disadvantaged kids. I've seen upper-middle-class parents lose their damn minds over AP and they have no idea why. They've bought into the notion that AP courses are essential to gaining access to the best universities. Yes, advanced placement classes can help the best students, but only when they're combined with an A average, great SAT (Scholastic Assessment Test) scores, and killer extracurricular activities.

High school–mandated "college courses"—even community college courses—can achieve the same goal. They give kids a better understanding of the academic behaviors that colleges look for and that kids need to succeed. Of course, the main reason that colleges require remediation is because kids come to college academically unprepared owing either to a lack of grounding in the subject or to behavioral issues. Exposure to college classes is one practical way to address both.

Schools like ours use college courses in the same way that upper-middle-class suburban schools use AP—to prove to colleges that our kids have what it takes to make it to, and graduate from, their campuses.

This happened with Emily, one of my Capital Prep kids. During senior year, she filled out her batch of college applications. Brigham Young University (BYU) was her top choice. Emily's SAT scores were solid, but not what Brigham Young typically expected for successful admissions.

I called up BYU personally. The admissions rep with whom I

spoke was polite and to the point. "I don't think Emily has what it takes to make it at BYU."

We went back and forth, debating various factors, and he told me that because of her less-than-stellar SAT scores, he didn't have faith that Emily could handle college work.

"Okay, if I prove that she can," I said, "will you reconsider?"

I produced her college transcript—sent proof that she's already been succeeding in college-level coursework.

Today, Emily is a BYU alum.

Even in the most affluent school districts, few schools have a full menu of AP courses—leaving parents at their wits' end. You know the type: we call them "helicopter" parents, always hovering, looking for one more way to prove that their kids have *it*. At schools that serve a low-income population, it's not the parents who have something to prove; it's the college counselors who have to show the world that their kids have it, *too*.

We built college into our school's DNA; we developed a partnership between Capital Prep and a community college, so this track is not optional: our kids automatically take college courses while still in high school. They typically graduate with as many as 60 college credits, which translates into a full two years of college completed. Here in Hartford, these same courses are open to all students. The only thing that parents need to do is to pay the nominal fee for a placement test, then enroll their kid.

Your child doesn't have to be enrolled at an early-college school like Capital Prep to use this effective strategy. Look around your city or town. Most community colleges offer courses that high school students can enroll in. Many four-year colleges offer them, too. But they cost a bit more and are typically tougher to get into.

At the end of the day, as a principal, I'm only concerned with what works in the real world. Yeah, the advanced placement system sounds great in theory. But community college courses serve the same purpose as AP while providing greater and more accessible benefits. And with community college credits, you don't necessarily have to blow away the competition. Even if your kid received a grade as low as a C, it doesn't disqualify the community college course from being transferable to a four-year college. The exams are based on an authentic college curriculum. Kids get the invaluable experience of being in college while receiving the supportive environment of their high school.

It's nice if your child gets an A on the advanced placement exam, but there's little hope of getting college credit for the course. By contrast, an A in a community college course usually equals 3 transferable college credits, a solid grade point average, and real proof that your kid has what it takes to succeed on a college campus. See you at graduation.

Time Keeps on Slippin'

THE CURRENT ACADEMIC calendar for public schools greatly contributes to the achievement gap. Why do kids need ten weeks off each summer? Do we honestly need research to underscore the obvious fact that students forget what they learn after not doing it for two and a half months?

Rest is the reason that we're given for the traditional summer vacation. Teachers say that the kids need a break from school. Yet there's no evidence that this is true. In fact, in my experience, most kids run out of things to do about seventy-two hours into the summer vacation. Let's be real: the only people who need rest are the teachers. Who wouldn't want the summer off to go to the beach, travel, do home improvements, hang out at barbecues, or romp around with their own kids? The only problem is that school was designed to educate kids, not to meet the scheduling whims of adults.

Consider the following. The traditional school year is too short to effectively educate kids. If a child loses almost three months of learning over his summer break, he spends the *first* three months of the next year doing over the *last* three months of school. And the problem is exacerbated by accommodations made for national and religious holidays such as Memorial Day, Thanksgiving, Christmas, Easter, Yom Kippur, Martin Luther

King Jr. Day, Presidents' Day, winter recess, spring break, professional development days, exams, and standardized and school testings. When we throw all those breaks in the loss column, our eight-month school year has dwindled to four months, with stops and starts almost every two weeks. No matter who's teaching (or learning), it is easy to see the implicit challenges this reduced learning time poses.

Besides supposed student "burnout," limited resources is the other reason given for sending children into communities where no less than 80 percent of adults aren't at home until well into the evening. Is money really the issue? Why does it cost more to educate a kid on July 23 than it does on January 23? The answer is because the teachers' unions don't want to work during the summer, so they compel school districts to pay much higher rates during those months. This is simply ridiculous.

If the teachers' unions kept their hourly rates constant, schools could stay open longer daily as well as annually. And municipalities and families would all benefit from keeping students in school longer. Fewer summer programs and police would be needed if teachers' unions would ring in the new millennium and stop extorting the community. Not every school would have to go year-round—that's not the point. For those schools that wish to extend the school calendar, unions have made the additional days too expensive. What's most peculiar about the unions' gouging is that most teachers end up working additional jobs during the summers anyway. So why does it have to cost so much?

The effects of summer vacation have been studied since 1906.

No one has ever proved the three-month break to be a necessity. The consistency of the results is what makes the tradition of long, costly summer breaks even more troubling. Police and parents all pay for teachers' time off. We all run around trying to find something meaningful for our kids to do so that we can keep our jobs, which allow us to pay taxes, which ensures that teachers get to straight chill all summer long. All children everywhere need access to year-round education. If y'all want the summers off, get a part-time job.

What in God's name is a nine-year-old supposed to do all summer for eight hours a day? Further, during the school year, what's that same nine-year-old supposed to do when he gets home at 2:10? Most of their families are at work. Hell, most of the world's families are at work except, of course, families headed by teachers. The current incompatibility between school and the country's employment patterns leads to entire neighborhoods full of unsupervised kids.

The United States is educating on an agrarian calendar even though less than 2 percent of the country makes a living from farming. We are using a calendar dictated by growing seasons to educate kids for a technically advanced economy. Elementary students are being educated for jobs and industries that have yet to be invented, and from June to September, they're home alone.

Teachers' unions are behind the continuation of this outdated calendar. If they really wanted to end this irrational schedule, it would end. No school board, principal, or city government would choose to have their children in the streets alone all afternoon and summer. Taxpayers who are already paying to keep their kids busy would leap at the chance to keep their schools running all year.

There's no justification for short days and long summers. Imagine if all physicians, hairdressers, and auto mechanics closed at 2:30 *every* afternoon and took off for three months *every* summer. Who on earth would sit still for that nonsense?

It's Not About the Benjamins

EDUCATION IS BY far the most expensive item on every community's budget. Yet our children's academic growth is limited by our adherence to outdated notions of *school*. No, not every kid cares about football games and proms. Not every kid fits in a uniform or desk. Not every kid can learn sitting in a traditional classroom. Every child learns how he or she learns. Don't we put all this money into education because we want children to learn? Isn't that why we waste months of an already short traditional school year doing standardized testing? Don't we want to know if kids are learning?

If the objective of public education is to educate children for an awaiting economy, then we have to part with the failing old way of doing things. Until we can prove that another traditional brick-and-mortar school is needed, there should be a public moratorium on building them. We owe it to our children to look at the countless strategies for educating children that have yet to be fully implemented.

We are all inextricably linked in this great big economy. Intuitively, we understand this. Most of us would admit that we learned more *doing* our job than we did training for it. We all remember as many life-changing bosses as teachers: men and women who changed the way we think and made it possible to earn a living and feed our family.

Leaders of the new school have the ideas; they just need the money. There are too many bright people who are interested in educational reform for us to limit them to a million square feet of urban schools. All over this country, there are teachers, preachers, business people, stay-at-home moms, and dads who have ideas that could be valuable contributions to improving education.

Charters, Magnets, and Tradition

THERE ARE ESSENTIALLY six categories of schools: private, charter, magnet, traditional (or neighborhood), home school, and the emerging market of online school.

I'm often asked which type of school I support.

I support any type of school that works.

No category of school works for all students and this is why I support full-on school choice. I'm not pro charter or magnet, I'm 100 percent pro good schools no matter the type. As a parent you intuitively know that even in your home, kids can be completely different. Each needs and wants something different from their school experience. But in helping them obtain it, you face two problems: first, knowing the difference between school types; and, second, gaining access.

The debate over which category of school is best at educating kids is, in a word, silly. It's like comparing bicycles to cars. No category of school is inherently more effective at educating children than the other. However, there are school *designs* that are more effective at educating kids than others.

Charter schools are schools that are publicly funded and privately operated. The term *private* is jarring to some. People often translate "private" as "for profit." But that's wrong. The United Way, Big Brothers, Big Sisters, and the Boys' and Girls' Clubs are all privately run organizations. They're not for profit. Most charter schools are operated by not-for-profit secular organizations.

Achievement First, the Harlem Children's Zone, Green Dot, YES Prep Academies, and KIPP (Knowledge Is Power Program) Academies are some of the most effective and largest charter school operators in the country. Each is a private not-for-profit organization. The postsecondary equivalent to privately run schools includes some of our oldest, most elite institutions: Harvard, Princeton, the University of Pennsylvania, and Stanford University. Each of these schools is a private not-for-profit organization. Each also receives public money to help run its operations. Each answers to its own board, rather than a school board or a board of regents. The colleges' boards, similar to charter schools' boards, create the institution's budget and designate spending priorities.

Magnet schools are very similar to charters, with a few distinctions. Magnets are public schools. Capital Prep is a magnet school. This means that I, like all other magnet school principals, work for the board of education. My boss is the superintendent of Hartford Public Schools. Magnets are also typically desegregated schools, opened to comply with court orders to desegregate.

There are more fundamental differences between charter/magnets and traditional neighborhood public schools. Charter/magnets have a theme, whereas a neighborhood school does not. Charters, more than magnets and traditional neighborhood schools, have the flexibility to hire and fire. Traditional neighborhood schools and magnets can do this as well; however, as I've explained, hiring and firing in a traditional school and in a magnet school is very costly and time consuming because both magnets and traditional neighborhood schools are public schools and often are staffed by union teachers.

Charter and magnet teachers and administrators have the option to work together to create their own themes and develop and/or select their curriculum. This is not the case for neighborhood schools. Their curriculum is developed off-site or purchased by central office staff without the input of the principal or his teachers. Charter and magnet school students are drawn from a region as opposed to a single neighborhood. Parents must apply to charter and magnet schools.

Neighborhood schools are aptly named because the kids who attend them must provide proof that they live in the neighborhood. All three types of school can have compacts outlining expectations. Charters and magnets often have more latitude to act when there are breaches in the compact. All three can ask students to leave for infractions, though neighborhood schools are most challenged in this respect.

Charter school teachers are typically nonunion and noncertified, unlike traditional and magnet schools. Charters, and to some degree magnet schools, set their own academic daily schedules, their own calendar, and develop their own staff job descriptions. Traditional public schools' daily schedule, calendar, and job descriptions are established through an agreement with the exclusive bargaining unit and cannot be augmented without the union's approval. For most charter and magnet schools, these decisions are made at the school level, taking into consideration the specific needs of the population of kids. In a traditional school system, these decisions are made for all schools through a contract with the union.

Charter and magnet school students are often as poor as—or poorer than—those who attend nearby neighborhood schools. Charter and magnet schools don't have any acceptance criteria and therefore a lottery is the method used to select students. Often educational performance is so seemingly "suburban" that people suspect charters and magnets of culling the best students from the applicant pool. They are wrong.

People have often asked me how we, at Capital Prep, *pick* our kids. Where do we find them? I tell them that we get them from the failing raggedy-ass schools. The presumption is that the only way that we could get our results is to cream—or select—the best kids from the most involved parents. This notion, while seemingly reasonable, is completely unfounded and untrue.

Why, then, this presumption? Plainly, it is a cop-out for those who could not educate the kids we've been able to send to college. Our results speak to other schools' ineptitude. Also, beneath the suggestion that we somehow have *different* kids are certain racist underpinnings.

Vouchers Are a Real Solution

VOUCHERS WORK. No, vouchers are not a panacea, but, in a different context, they worked to close dangerous public housing projects and open up new suburban neighborhoods to poor people. Those vouchers are called Section 8. The same can happen for poor children in our failed schools.

The vouchers must be real and absolute. Set them at a maximum of 80 percent of the state's most expensive per pupil expenditure. Combine that with parents' income to determine the minimum allotment to a family, just like the Feds do for financial aid. The children will carry that money with them, just as Section 8 vouchers are disbursed for housing, Medicare and Medicaid, food stamps, and Pell Grants—all are public vouchers for private goods and services.

Failing districts must be repurposed so that their role is to disburse vouchers and monitor school progress. Failed districts should not hire teachers or administrators. They should not set curricula. Their persistent failure in these areas is more than reason enough to relieve them of this opportunity to screw up again. All these elements of school administration must be handled at the school level. Parents, students, community boards, faculty, and staff can decide what is best for their schools.

The standards for success must be set against those of average suburban districts. Not the top, not the bottom—the average. This establishes reasonable expectations for students, staff, and families. Every child needs at least an average suburban education to gain access to, and to contribute to, the modern economy.

Schools that don't meet or exceed the criteria for growth and success must be closed. The free market must extend to education. In this model, superintendents will serve roles similar to those of federal Department of Education directors. Their staffs will set parameters and measures progress toward success.

When vouchers are instituted and the role of school districts changes, each school will establish its own labor agreements, schedules, curriculum, themes, and cultures. This ain't educational anarchy. It's truly American. This is standard among the private schools to which people like Barack and Michelle Obama have always sent their kids. Only the poor cannot choose their own schools. Only the poor have to participate in an educational structure that is a proven failure. That may be America, but it ain't American.

Vouchers can no longer be dismissed as right-wing Republican propaganda. Providing all families with the opportunity to choose from educational options that suit their needs will both inspire and support good new schools. Will some people cheat the system? Yep. But what do you call taking $120 million of taxpayers' money to build a school that graduates fewer than 30 percent of its kids? Will fleeing students cause many of the schools to fail? Probably. But would that aggregated failure be any more profound than the one already staring us in the face? The only good thing about nearly absolute failure is that it can't get much worse.

The middle and upper classes already have vouchers. They're called good jobs. Meanwhile, impoverished people must settle for an impoverished education. But the debilitating cycle of poverty *can* be ended when education is equally distributed among the poor and well-to-do. Vouchers will achieve this equalization.

We Know What Works

THERE IS ABSOLUTELY no mystery about what needs to be done to improve schools. We've known for generations. Successful schools and academic support programs are designed to develop relationships with children, identify strengths, and challenge students through a combination of high expectations and high support.

I've already talked about the elements that will make running effective schools possible in the new millennium: great teachers and great lesson plans, committed principals, a lengthened school calendar, the use of technology, and an updated curriculum. There are also additional characteristics that have been known for decades but haven't yet made their way into the mainstream.

These characteristics are apparent in private, parochial, magnet, charter, and, to some degree, traditional neighborhood schools as well as in part-time out-of-school programs including, but not limited to, Upward Bound, Prep for Prep, A Better Chance, and Posse. Before exploring these traits, let's start by defining success.

Parents are often lulled into believing that their suburban school is a good school. It's relatively safe, the kids seem as happy as kids can be, and the high school's top 10 percent go on to elite colleges. Test scores are generally good and, in many cases, the parents themselves have fond memories of attending the same school.

For me, and for many of today's education reformers, these characteristics represent a low threshold by which to measure academic success. The types of superlative schools that we read about in the media, those whose stories make us equal parts inspired and envious, would never accept this as the measure of their success.

Successful schools and programs see the success of a *few* as failure. They expect all children to go to top colleges, participate in high-level learning, or otherwise realize their potential. That being the case, they design the academic experience to account for all students, not just the few—the brilliant, the outstanding, the elite handful—who would have arguably made it no matter where they were educated.

The country's best schools and programs develop a sense of family. This feeling I have of belonging is driven by the combination of design and personnel. Each successful learning experience presumes that kids are going to need guidance out of the thicket that is childhood. Likewise, it's clear that the parents are also going to need some guidance. Successful academic experiences assign every child an *adviser*. An adviser is typically a teacher in the case of a school, or a mentor in the case of an out-of-school program. No matter what they're called, the function of this person is to support student and family as they go through the process. This mentoring includes, but is by no means limited to, encouraging effective study habits, monitoring student performance, and helping in the selection of courses, and eventually, majors.

In traditional schools, parents receive a progress report at week nine of a sixteen-week marking period. By that time, if your son is getting a B-minus, he's going to finish the class with a B-minus. It's effectively too late for you or anyone to help your child at that point. By keeping parents in the dark, schools fail parents who want to support their children. The system isn't designed for you or your child. It's designed for convenience. Printing up progress reports is often too time consuming in those settings—there are too many kids, and hence too much extra work for all the staff. Tough luck, Chuck. Just keep hounding your son's algebra teacher and hope that she calls you back before he fails.

Fortunately, an advisory system doesn't cost more money. It's implemented in programs that serve America's most disadvantaged students as well as in the most elite private schools. It works because every child is accounted for and all parents can stay on top of their kids' grades and emotional issues.

Every school in America could—and should—have an advisory system. All that's required is to assign every teacher a small group of kids. Many schools have homeroom and study hall. Instead of just being places where kids catch up on homework or line up a date, these locations could be where a teacher engages the students in meaningful check-ins. She could ask the students to take out their school agendas. She could walk around to make sure they're all signed. She could develop group activities that turn into teen discussions. She could celebrate every kid's birthdays with a $15 pizza. She could turn every meeting into a study group session. The point is that all the essential components are already in place. The teacher is there, the kids are there—why not make a simple adjustment and improve the educational process?

Well, of course, there *is* a reason.

For Capital Prep to assign a teacher fifteen students, to ask a teacher to act in the capacity of adviser, I must get an addendum to the teacher's contract. You see, when a teacher touches base with kids, calls home to inform parents how the kids are doing—if this occurs during a period in which the teacher isn't teaching—the teachers' unions view it as an additional *duty,* for which the community must pay. Even though advising occurs *during* the school day, it's outside the typical teachers' contract. Conversely, advising is a basic element of teachers' responsibilities in successful schools and programs.

Teachers in the most effective academic experiences are *busy!* At the elite private schools they call it the *triple threat.* Every teacher coaches, teaches, and advises—in addition to her evening and weekend responsibilities. When the kids are at a boarding school, of course, these responsibilities grow.

Traditional schools are so different from successful elite schools, both public and private. Teachers in traditional schools simply don't have to work as hard to be considered successful. These schools are designed to make the teacher's day easier. Elite schools embed students and teachers in the experience. In traditional schools, teachers have teachers' lounges, private and closed even to administrators or, in some cases, even to other departments. In the elite successful schools, on the other hand, teachers have to eat with the kids, have to relate to them in non-classroom settings. At boarding schools, staff and students even live together—they have ice cream socials in their apartments. The best schools understand that teachers have to work their asses off to get the most out of kids, and to do this, the teachers must be more than just the person at the front of the class. That's why they have to coach, advise, and teach—for starters.

The best academic experiences are organized around a theme. A theme is a pronounced philosophy. No one theme is better than another in foretelling a school's capacity to prepare students. The purpose of the theme is to provide direction for teaching and learning. It aligns hiring, evaluations, and student expectations. When your theme is science, you hire people who are good at or have a respect for science. You look for people excited by the prospect of producing young scientists. You can evaluate your school's effectiveness by its ability to produce students who have a well-developed capacity for science. The theme is the purpose that the academic experience fulfills.

Too many schools are just *schools*. They don't teach anything in particular and, as a result, they don't seem to be teaching anything at all. Teachers are going through the motions. There is no passion, no creativity. Everything is cookie-cutter. Math is math and science is science. Assignments are not coordinated in any way; no consideration is made for the workloads kids have in their different subjects. A well-executed theme is truly interdisciplinary, brings the academic experience together for the staff and students, and helps both staff and students to uncover meaning in teaching and learning.

People know what to expect in successful schools. When you apply to Choate Rosemary Hall in Wallingford, Connecticut, you know what you are getting. There are no negotiations. If you don't like it—peace. The same is true with the National Cathedral School, Urban Prep, or any of the KIPP (Knowledge Is Power Program) schools. Their success is in their model. They will all look to improve and grow, but change? Nah. If the fit isn't right for your child, you should just find another school.

Teachers at these theme-oriented elite schools know what is expected and they either comply or get fired. Students and parents know as well, and if they don't like it, they can get out, too. Not every school is for everybody. This cannot be overstated.

Schools that produce well-prepared students have little in common with most of America's academic offerings. Any resemblance to the typical American public school is unintended.

AT THIS STAGE, I'm sorry to say, America's schools cannot be reformed.

A basic premise of reformation is that there still exists a foundation that can be built on. That isn't the case. Public education needs a *transformation* rather than a *reformation*. And some of what will need to be done has yet to be discovered or invented.

There is, however, a well-established body of knowledge regarding what's proved practical and effective.

When we started Capital Prep, we went looking for what *works*. We found it, employed it, and now *we* work. There is absolutely no excuse for our nation's schools failing to meet our expectations, failing to get the most out of our students, or failing to protect our country from the demise that follows generations of underpreparation.

The last great school has not been opened. Today, education

has gone digital. It streams into iPads over 4G networks. It rests at a kitchen table. It's in the 'hood and in the swankiest suburbs. We know how to educate. We are a nation with thousands of effective schools. The problem is that we have tens of thousands of failed schools *mis*educating tens of millions.

But I'm not pessimistic. In fact, I'm inspired by what the future holds for American children. The only thing that stands in the way of our children's success is the limits of our adult imagination. When we open up our minds to the options that already exist, thousands more children will love school and light up our future.

Knowing what works is half the battle. Implementing is the second half. Push has come to shove. Somebody has got to do something. Somebody who looks just like you, lives in your neighborhood, and sends their kids to your kid's school. Somebody who now knows what works and what doesn't. Somebody who loves our children's future more than our adults' careers.

COURAGE IS often overemphasized. Sometimes the greatest deeds in modern history were merely normal reactions to circumstances. Over time, a simple act—steeped in moral character—attains the stature of myth.

Here's a parable I often like to quote.

There was once a king who stood upon the banks of a mighty river with his daughter, the princess. His most courageous warriors stood on the opposing bank.

The king knew that he would not live forever and so he wanted a prince who could lead his kingdom. He issued a decree: "I am looking for a brave warrior, a leader among men!" A roar rose over the raging rapids of the mighty crocodile-infested river. "I have a challenge! Whoever shall swim across this river shall have all of my riches and my daughter's hand in marriage or anything else his heart desires." The princess was a beautiful and brilliant young woman; the king possessed untold riches in gold and diamonds; but there was that river—that raging, crocodile-invested river. . . .

The warriors looked at one another, exchanged wary glances, and suddenly—splash! A hole appeared in their ranks. They noticed one of their own, a young warrior, in the river, fighting desperately to make the crossing. As the crocs slithered into the water, headed toward the young man, a collective shout sounded over both banks: the young man swam! His arms pumped, his back flexed, his legs churned the water like propellers. The roar grew louder as the young man disappeared into the undertow and emerged again—pursued by the razor-toothed, prehistoric-looking reptiles. With one last burst he catapulted out of the river and onto the bank, grasping the hand of the king himself, who'd reached down to pull the young man out.

The young warrior stood for just a moment until, overcome with emotion and fatigue, his hands dropped onto his knees. The king at that moment raised the young man's hand high into the air. In a booming voice, he announced, "Young man, you made it. You succeeded against all odds. You may have all of my riches and my daughter's hand in marriage."

The young man looked at the king and the warriors back on the distant bank before speaking. "Your Highness," he said, "you are a wealthy and benevolent man"—his chest heaved as he paused to catch his breath—"and your daughter is beautiful, indeed. . . ." He hunched over and, now facing the cheering warriors he had left on the far bank, shouted:

"All I want is the *fool* that pushed me into the water!"

YOU'VE BEEN PUSHED. You know what works.

Now *swim* like your life depends on it.

Making a Living—
Making a Life

ON THE MORNING before Christmas 2010, I received a text from arguably the most influential educator in America. The text simply asked if I was available to talk. I said that I was and I received a call within a few minutes.

Since I started writing *Push Has Come to Shove,* my life has been completely blown off the hinges. I still have the same small group of friends. I keep in touch with them—though not as much. I still leave my house in the half-darkness, picking up Capital Prep students who don't have a ride to school—though not as much. I'm still the principal of Capital Prep—though not in the same way I used to be.

When we opened Capital Prep in August 2004, we had two weeks to hire an entire staff. We were in a temporary, very cramped space at the community college, and certain folks there treated us quite poorly. The district fought every idea we had. My bosses—yes, there were many—agreed on one thing. They all thought we were nuts and were going to fail miserably.

By December 24, 2010, Capital Prep could boast some of the highest scores in reading and writing on the state's standardized

tests. This placed us among the elite, not just in the city of Hartford, but throughout Connecticut; our students scored 97 percent proficient in reading and 100 percent proficient in writing.
Since opening, we'd sent 100 percent of Capital Prep graduates
to four-year colleges. We'd been featured in CNN's *Black in America 2*—seen by over 14 million viewers. We were going into our
fourth consecutive year on *U.S. News & World Report*'s ranking of
Top High Schools in America. Hell, despite our small size, even
our athletic teams were dominant, winning five consecutive conference championships in cross country, three in girls' basketball,
and one in boys' basketball. We even had the number one men's
basketball player in the nation, and the number one scorer in the
state.

We'd gone from a cramped floor in the community college to
a breathtaking $42.5 million state-of-the-art campus. We'd been
visited by hundreds of educators, parents, politicians from all
over the country, and quite a few celebrities. We'd been sought
out by educators from three countries and a TV crew from South
Korea, which filmed a documentary on us. Yes, our first six years
had gone pretty well.

But by December 24, 2010, the exciting life I'd promised my
wife had officially spun out of control. I often felt that I was in
that famous *I Love Lucy* episode where Lucille Ball stands at the
candy-factory conveyer belt, trying to find something to do with
all of the chocolates streaming toward her. What I thought would
be a one on-off with CNN turned into a job as CNN's education
contributor, complete with a weekly feature on *Anderson Cooper
360*. I replaced Reagan's former secretary of education, William

Bennett. Then *Essence* magazine asked me to be its education contributor—the magazine's first. This was followed by an invitation from Walt Disney World asking me to be a part of a huge annual event that they do. In between, I'd appeared on MSNBC and Fox. Then there was the speaking—50,000 miles in the spring of 2010 alone—and the job offers, superintendent's gigs across the country. Those first six years were the best of times and the worst of times.

I lost touch with my family in 2010. My sons and wife spent the better part of every week together with me Skyping in from wherever I was—assuming I could get Internet or it wasn't past their bedtimes. I lost touch with my school. My academic dean, Rich Beganski, and a few key staff really stepped up. Even as the school thrived, I lost the depth that I once had with my staff, and my friends just stopped expecting to see me unless it was on TV. I often wondered how things could be going so well and I could feel so damn messed up.

I had plans for 2011–2012 to be different. I all but shut down my speaking. Whatever wasn't booked wasn't going to happen. I said no to all offers and decided to stay with the school I love. I coached my eldest son Mason's football team and, although I missed the last three games because of travel, I was a dad again. I liked that. I also decided to open an elementary school on campus and enroll my two sons, plus some of my staff's kids—getting back to basics. Then Christmas Eve 2010 came.

The conversation was simple. "Steve, we need you to run one of America's most important districts. Please consider it."

That was it.

I said I would listen to the offer.

BARELY AN HOUR later I'm upstairs, talking out the details with my publicist Yusuf Salaam, telling him that I just want to stay in my house with my kids, continue to run my school, when suddenly my wife and eldest son start screaming for me to come down-stairs.

Never in my life have I heard them shout so loudly, with such shrillness.

I shoot to my feet. My phone drops and shatters on the floor as I run downstairs. When I turn the corner, I see my wife hold-ing my motionless five-year-old in her arms—rocking, pleading for him to wake up. I take Walker in my arms and tell her to call 911.

My thoughts are racing: just a year earlier Walker had been caught in a flash flood in which he'd almost drowned—now *this*.

I try frantically to get Walker to respond. In my ear Mason, eight, keeps yelling, "I'm not going to have a little brother!"

I place Walker flat on the carpet, wipe his face clear, and begin to administer CPR.

"One and two and three and *blow*—"

Nothing. His lips are turning blue. He seems to be choking on his own mucus. Hearing the wailing of my wife and son, I pray for my son to open his eyes.

"Please wake up, Walker. Daddy really loves you and your brother is very worried." Nothing. I tell him I knew what I got him for Christmas. Still nothing.

"One and two and three and . . ."

Surreal and overwhelming as it all is, one thought squeezes in—why in the hell had I been going so *hard* all the time? In all that I'd done recently, I'd lost my way. The calls to help other children had taken me away from my own kids. I'd said that I'd hoped that I would touch enough lives so that one day when my sons really resented me, they'd meet someone who'd thank them for loaning me out and would tell them that their dad was a good dude who answered a call to save children.

To do what I do, the way I've done it—yes, of course, you've got to have an ego—I must *believe* that I can change the world, and, at times, I feel as though I have. I've inspired and saved the lives of people I know and those I will never meet—but none of that matters now. My little boy is losing consciousness next to the Christmas tree. I have never felt so powerless, so humble.

I hear myself screaming, pleading, still trying CPR.

"One and two and three and—"

Suddenly, Walker shoves me in the chest. I wipe the mucus from his face and he pushes me again. That's my little fire-breather! Frantically watching and begging for the ambulance to arrive, my wife asks, "Is he breathing?" I tell her that he is.

The paramedics arrive—they conclude that Walker suffered a febrile seizure—and rush him to the hospital. Sitting in the back of the speeding ambulance, jolting back and forth, I ask myself if being away so much was worth it. I mentally rifle through all the plane tickets, meetings, and late nights. Then the call, less than an hour ago—the job offer—to which I'd promised I'd listen.

I hate that I've missed so much. I also understand now, more than ever, this *calling*.

I SET OUT TO make a life—not just a living. When you make a living, you pay your bills. When you make a life, you pay your debt. A lot became clear to me in that ambulance on Christmas Eve 2010. One thing that I cannot figure out is why my little boy made it.

I'd like to think that He granted us mercy because my family has committed to making a life. I don't get to do any of this without my wife and kids supporting me. So *maybe* we had a few chips in the bank—ones I spent on Christmas Eve.

Today I'm more focused than ever. I know that mine must be a life of purpose. I've seen the frailty of human life. Fortunately, my son Walker has now fully recovered.

"Today is a gift," as the old saying goes. "That's why they call it the *present.* " After living through my boy's Christmas seizure, those words never rang so true.

I love my life and am grateful for those in it. I know that each one of us is here to do something. I believe this is my season to educate. This carries the responsibility of creating new paradigms, fighting the old guard. This means knowing the difference between receiving a call from someone important, an offer to make a living—and answering The Call, to make a life.

Appendix A

The following is the American Federation of Teachers 2011 Connecticut Agenda. Lively reading it is not. I include it here so you'll note that the union's political agenda makes no mention of students or learning!

2011 AFT CONNECTICUT LEGISLATIVE AGENDA

The overall goal of the AFT Connecticut legislative agenda is to advocate for legislation and a state budget that will protect and improve the rights, safety, and quality of life for all AFT Connecticut members.

The 2011 Session is a long one. It will convene on January 5th and adjourn on June 8th. The following are AFT Connecticut's union-wide priorities:

- Working for a fair budget that includes adequate funding for state services, PK-16 education & higher education, collective bargaining agreements and binding arbitration awards and all state funded pensions, and acute care hospital funding.

- Preventing any effort to reduce services and jobs by capping taxes or spending at either the state or municipal level.

- Fighting efforts to privatize state or municipal services, including public education.

- Stopping efforts to weaken the binding arbitration process for state employees, teachers and municipal employees.

- Monitoring the legislative recommendations and universal health care plan designed by the SustiNet Board of Directors.

Our union will also work on the following legislative issues that affect each constituency group during the 2011 Legislative Session:

PRE-K–12 COUNCIL

Oppose "money follows the child" education funding schemes or any other such proposal that would move dollars away from the neediest public schools to those that do not provide opportunity equally to all students.

- Block efforts to use public funds to establish private school vouchers and provide tax credits for businesses that contribute to private schools.

- Secure funding for CommPACT schools in FY 2012 and FY 2013 and reallocate secured funds so that all monies flow to the University of Connecticut's Neag School of Education.

- Stop efforts to supplant art and music teachers by providing credit to students who complete programs at private institutions.

- Require charter schools to produce student achievement levels that are substantially greater than those at surrounding traditional public schools.

- Monitor efforts to alter certification requirements.

- Watch attempts to alter teacher evaluation systems without teacher input.

- Monitor State Department of Education legislative proposals that may negatively affect AFT Connecticut members, such as:
  - Efforts to create "Crandall Schools" and other Sheff compliance initiatives
  - Raising the Kindergarten age
  - Reducing reporting requirements

- Monitor recommendations from the General Assembly's Individualized Education Plan Task Force.

- Monitor recommendations from the General Assembly's and Governor Rell's Achievement Gap Task Forces.

- Restore funding for school resource officers in technical high schools.

- Monitor potential tweaks to school governance council statute.

PSRP COUNCIL

- Protect the State Department of Education's Paraprofessional Professional Development Advisory Council and restore its funding.

- Reduce the number of hours full-time paraprofessionals are required to work in order to be eligible to receive Family Medical Leave (FMLA) benefits.

HEALTHCARE COUNCIL

- Enact legislation to prevent and respond to incidents of workplace violence in hospitals and other healthcare settings.

- Require that every school building have a school nurse.

- Establish a School Nurse Professional Development Advisory Council.

- Require school administrators and superintendents to enforce statutory mandates that require children to be vaccinated before they are allowed to attend public school.

- Block attempts to allow physicians assistants to use radiology equipment without full radiology training.

- Monitor and evaluate legislative proposals surrounding Certificate of Need reform.

STATE EMPLOYEES COUNCIL

- Monitor legislative recommendations from the Program Review & Investigations Committee's study on Whistleblower Complaints.

- Support efforts to establish the Connecticut Healthcare Partnership Act, i.e., the pooling bill.

- Pass card check recognition for public sector workers who choose to unionize (pending approval of the AFL-CIO Legislative Committee).

- Evaluate recommendations from the Commission on Enhancing Agency Outcomes, including reform of the Office of Administrative Hearings and consolidation of state agencies.

- Monitor legislation that addresses workplace bullying.

RETIREE COUNCIL

- Establish dues check-off from pension checks of retired teachers.

- Mandate health insurance policies to cover $2,000 in hearing aid benefit within a sixty-month period to all insureds over the age of 55.

Appendix B: We Are Capital Prep!

There is a seventy-two-foot banner hanging from the rafters in the gymnasium of the Capital Preparatory Magnet School in Hartford, Connecticut. The large, burnt-orange letters dominate the room.

"We are Capital Prep!"

These words exist to remind the school's 540 students—more than 86 percent of them of color and 70 percent of this group have been deemed "disadvantaged" by the state of Connecticut—that they are part of something bigger than themselves.

We are a brash family of educators, parents, and children who dreamed that college would be available to all children. We are a Grade K–12, year-round, college preparatory social justice school that is unapologetically successful. Since we opened our doors in 2005, we've sent 100 percent of our graduates to four-year colleges. We have an average daily attendance of more than 96 percent, and we have never had a student drop out. Each year since our second year of operation we have been named to *U.S. News & World Report*'s "Top High Schools in America" list. CNN, Fox, and MSNBC have all come to see us as a success story.

Being Capital Prep is a lifestyle. We are crisp, crested white shirts, silk ties, and blue blazers for our high school boys. We are crisp, crested white shirts and plaid kilts for all our girls. We are disciplined classrooms; well-mannered children in a building that was remolded to represent a sense of purpose.

The Capital Prep lifestyle is as much what we are not as what we are.

We are not excuses. Many of our students are poor where money is the measure, yet every single one is rich in promise and potential. Our faculty is gay, straight, religious, and agnostic, but when the day begins they are teachers who must send children to college.

We are not a school that is afraid of children nor are we interested in meeting their ever-growing whims. We know that the lives of our children are tough but, no, we still do not understand why a kid didn't do his homework. We know that almost 80 percent of our children live without fathers but, no, we still don't see that as cause to disrupt our classes. We know most of our children come to us four grades behind but, no, we still will not accept that college isn't in their future.

We are Capital Prep! is an answer. Why do we care about the details? Because we are Capital Prep. Why does every kid have to go to college? We are Capital Prep. Why do you go through so many teachers? Why does our staff constantly give kids rides, stock their rooms with food, get angry when parents don't come to games or children forget to wear their belt to school? Simply because we are Capital Prep.

Can we lay claim to being the best school in the country? Nah. Not yet. But we are damn sure pursuing that goal. It's this pursuit that makes us who we are. We have a constantly questioning, never-good-enough obsession with maximizing the potential of all our students. We are competitive with other schools and respectful of what they have done. From teacher to teacher, there is competition and respect for accomplishments but no tolerance for mediocrity. Most of the founders still work at the school, and all of us know what it took for us to be where we are. Therefore, nothing less than the best will do.

Finally, we are Capital Prep because we love kids. At the end of the day we do not like all of them, but tomorrow will wash all of that clean. Standing ready to greet every child, every day, we want them to know that they are loved. We want them to feel welcomed home, and we want them to know that a new day has presented them with the opportunity to work their asses off. This is the greatest expression of our love. High expectations are the only expectations that we have. When we say that "We are Capital Prep," we are making a statement, answering questions, and declaring a way of life. No apologies. No excuses. No further explanation needed.

Acknowledgments

Thank you, Mason. From the first breath you've been my light. I love you so much that I didn't think I had any more love to give, then your little fire-breathing brother came out screaming. Walker, I've never met a person with more self-confidence, and you're five. No man should have so much, this much to love, and these two children to love—but I do. You make me feel rich, overwhelmed, and embarrassed that I have so much. Now you have everything I wanted as a child. If we were classmates, I'd be jealous. As your father I'm humbled, proud. You have a head start. You are both so blessed. You have so much to learn and contribute.

Lalani, look at what we've done. They are beautiful, aggravating, funny, and smart. Typically, I'd take credit, but we have company. Marriage is a test. Love is a journey, and happiness is a pursuit. Which means we are studying as we find our bearings and give chase to the only thing worth having: happiness. I love you, us, and the life we are building.

Mom, thank you. Starting as far back as we did, it sure feels good to be winning. Only you believed when it seemed unbelievable. Look around, there are no more doubters. Enjoy your day in the sun, at the spa, up front with the wind at your back.

Dad, dude, seriously? You've got to do better. Seriously. This ain't fly. You and I are too old for this. When Walker has to ask you who you are, it's gotta get you thinking and living more seriously. No more excuses, you can write the final chapter.

Yusuf, Rich "B" Beganski, Fult, and Cle: together we've built something to talk about and a stage on which to talk. Thank you.

Capital Prep students, parents, and staff: you've given me purpose and a reason to wake up each day. I exist because you've made it so. Thank you.

Soledad O'Brien: you amaze me. You've kept your word from day one—that means a lot. Thank you.

Dreamers, friends, and detractors: your names and our interactions combine to become inspirations. Thank you.

Bonnie Solow: you're awesome. You are responsible for *Push Has Come to Shove.* Your nurturing and push have taken a passion and transformed it into my favorite book. Thank you.

"Big" Doug Century: thank you for signing up for this. We've ripped the cover off this one. Good lookin' out.

Rick Horgan: your mentoring and willingness to piss me off has made me a better writer. You are the mark on the wall to which I now write. Thank you for believing in me enough to push me to be better.

Then there's the entire Crown Publishing Group/Random House family, led by publisher Molly Stern, Rachel Rokicki, Nathan Roberson, and Julie Cepler. It's a joy to work with you all.

About the Author

DR. STEVE PERRY is in a hurry to transform the educational experience for *all* children. Born into poverty, he believes that success in life is determined by where you end, not where you start. It's this philosophy that inspired him, early on, to transform the lives of poor and minority children by providing them with access to a college education, and, more recently, has inspired him to bring his ideas and passion to children everywhere, no matter what their socioeconomic or academic background.

In 1998 Dr. Perry founded ConnCAP, the Connecticut Collegiate Awareness Program, at Capital Community College. For a period of six years, the program sent 100 percent of its low-income, first-generation graduates to four-year colleges. Then in 2004 Capital Preparatory Magnet School was established in Hartford, Connecticut's lowest-performing district. Since its inception, that school also has sent 100 percent of its graduates to four-year colleges.

Capital Prep has been recognized by *U.S. News & World Report* as one of America's Best High Schools. Dr. Perry's uncompromising, no-excuses approach to designing the ideal educational experience for children led to his being featured on CNN's documentary *Black in America* and from there to an official role as a weekly education contributor on the network. His "Perry's

Principles" and other reportage, regularly seen on both *Anderson Cooper 360* and *American Morning*, tackles the most contentious issues being debated in American education.

Dr. Perry has been a columnist for *Essence* magazine, and before writing *Push Has Come to Shove* he self-published several books, including the bestselling *Man Up!* He is also a nationally sought-after speaker who has appeared on hundreds of radio and television broadcasts and at education and cultural forums around the country.

To learn more about Dr. Steve Perry, go to www.dr-steveperry .com.

STEVE PERRY is available for select readings and lectures. To inquire about a possible appearance, please contact the Random House Speakers Bureau at rhspeakers@randomhouse.com.